C0-AOD-114

BUCKNELL REVIEW

The Arts, Society, Literature

STATEMENT OF POLICY

BUCKNELL REVIEW is a scholarly interdisciplinary journal. Each issue is devoted to a major theme or movement in the humanities or sciences, or to two or three closely related topics. The editors invite heterodox, orthodox, and speculative ideas and welcome manuscripts from any enterprising scholar in the humanities and sciences.

This journal is a member of the Conference of Editors of Learned Journals

BUCKNELL REVIEW
A Scholarly Journal of Letters, Arts, and Sciences

Contributors should send manuscripts with a self-addressed stamped envelope to the Editor, Bucknell University, Lewisburg, Pennsylvania 17837.

BUCKNELL REVIEW

THE ARTS, SOCIETY, LITERATURE

Edited by
HARRY R. GARVIN

Special Associate Editor This Issue
JAMES M. HEATH

LEWISBURG
BUCKNELL UNIVERSITY PRESS
LONDON AND TORONTO: ASSOCIATED UNIVERSITY PRESSES

Associated University Presses
440 Forsgate Drive
Cranbury, NJ 08512

Associated University Presses
25 Sicilian Avenue
London WC1A 2QH
England

Associated University Presses
2133 Royal Windsor Drive
Unit 1
Mississauga, Ontario
Canada L5J 1K5

Library of Congress Cataloging in Publication Data
Main entry under title:

The Arts, society, literature.

(Bucknell review; v. 29, no. 1)
Contents: Roland and Romanesque: Biblical iconography in The song of Roland / William R. Cook, Ronald B. Herzman—Wordsworth, Coleridge, and Turner / James A. W. Heffernan—Alexander Pope and picturesque land-scape / James R. Aubrey—[etc.]
1. Arts and society—Addresses, essays, lectures.
I. Garvin, Harry Raphael, 1917– II. Heath, James M. III. Series.
AP2.B887 vol. 29, no. 1 051s [700'.1'03] 83-46177
[NX180.S6]
ISBN 0-8387-5080-X

(Volume XXIX, Number 1)

Printed in the United States of America

Contents

Recent Issues of BUCKNELL REVIEW

Phenomenology, Structuralism, Semiology
Twentieth-Century Poetry, Fiction, Theory
Literature and History
New Dimensions in the Humanities and Social Sciences
Women, Literature, Criticism
The Arts and Their Interrelations
Shakespeare: Contemporary Approaches
Romanticism, Modernism, Postmodernism
Theories of Reading, Looking, and Listening
Literature, Arts, and Religion
Literature and Ideology
Science and Literature
The American Renaissance: New Dimensions
Rhetoric, Literature, and Interpretation

Notes on Contributors

JAMES R. AUBREY: Teaches at the United States Air Force Academy. His interest in the visual arts has evolved from studies in the eighteenth century. Scholarly publications include an essay on Beowulf.

WILLIAM R. COOK: Teaches at State University of New York, Geneseo. Professional interests: Medieval history, especially church history; the Bible as history; interdisciplinary Medieval studies. Publications in Hussite theology, Medieval spirituality. Recent articles on negotiations between the Hussites, the Holy Roman Emperor, and the Roman Church, 1427–36; analogies between Cluniac sculpture and Cistercian writings; the tympanum of Neuilly-en-Donjon.

LEO PAUL S. DE ALVAREZ: Teaches at the University of Dallas. He edited and contributed an essay to *Abraham Lincoln, The Gettysburg Address and American Constitutionalism* (Irving, Texas: University of Dallas Press, 1976). He has translated Machiavelli's *Prince* (Irving, Texas: University of Dallas Press, 1981) and is presently completing a commentary to accompany the third edition of that work. His essay on *Timon of Athens,* part of his projected book titled *Shakespeare's Athens,* is published in *Shakespeare as Political Thinker,* ed. John Alvis and Thomas G. West (Durham, N.C.: Carolina Academic Press, 1981).

KRIN GABBARD: Teaches at State University of New York, Stony Brook. Major professional interests: interrelations among the arts, including film. Articles on Homer, Robert Browning, John Updike, Ingmar Bergman, Robert Wise, and Alfred Hitchcock. Current project: a book on Robert Altman.

JAMES M. HEATH: Chairman of the Department of Classics at Bucknell University. Professional interests in Greek and Roman history, literature, and philology. Associate Editor of *Bucknell Review* since 1976.

JAMES A. W. HEFFERNAN: Teaches at Dartmouth College. Author of *Wordsworth's Theory of Poetry,* of numerous articles on Wordsworth, and of *Writing: A College Handbook* (New York: Norton, 1982). Currently working on a book-length study of the relation between English Romantic poetry and painting.

RONALD B. HERZMAN: Teaches at State University of New York, Geneseo. Professional interests: Medieval literature, especially Dante and Chaucer, and interdisciplinary Medieval studies. Publications mostly on Dante and Chaucer. Recent articles on sacramental inversion in Inferno 19 (with William A. Stephany), Inferno 27 (a note on St. Eustace), and an approach to the Miller's and Reeve's Tales. In progress (with William R. Cook): a manuscript, *On the Shoulders of Giants: An Introduction to the Medieval World View.*

JAMES H. KAVANAGH: Teaches at Princeton University. He has published essays on Marxist critical theory, modern fiction, and contemporary film. He serves as an advisory editor for *Praxis,* and in the editorial collective of *Social Text.*

LUCIAN KRUKOWSKI: Teaches at Washington University in St. Louis. His paintings have been exhibited nationally. Scholarly articles on the arts. He is completing a book on the ontology of artworks.

STEPHEN P. SMITH: Teaches at Idaho State University, where he specializes in modern poetry and eighteenth-century British literature. Currently engaged in a study of modern Scottish literature, especially the poetry of Hugh MacDiarmid and its relationship to the language and nationalist problems of Scotland.

Introduction

A generation ago, the association of the arts, literature, and society in a common scholarly effort seemed unusual, daring, unorthodox. In the 1980s, it is no longer easy for scholars to establish and defend traditional and simple categories for disciplines. Responsible critics face the more difficult problem of establishing the ground rules on which to base their studies of those works or phenomena which cannot easily be categorized as simply literary, fine arts, or societal. Such critics have also to determine a basis or stance of authority from which to conduct investigations that involve fields in which they may not lay claim to professional competence. The contemporary tendency to value specialization above general abilities clashes with a striving to transcend the narrowness of disciplines by a synthesis that resembles the liberal arts generalism of an earlier age. But since that generalism too easily turns out to be superficial, contemporary critics and scholars are wary of simplistic formulas that merely sound profound.

The scholars and critics who write in this issue of *Bucknell Review* present examples of responsible approaches to integrating various disciplines, relying on their professional competence in one or more areas but not denying the limitations they face in exploring territory beyond their own domain. Although the articles are arranged in groups that pair particular "disciplines," the principal focus of the issue, the editors believe, is the synthesis of certain themes and questions common to the various combinations of articles. Addressing these concerns provides a way to seek interconnections among the various areas.

Common to all fields, for example, is a concern for definition, for stating as precisely as possible the meaning of terms used to characterize phenomena not limited to a single field. James Heffernan approaches the long-discussed question of how to define *Romanticism* in a way that breaks out of the traditional hermeneutical circle. Earlier critics constructed a concept of Romanticism based on analogies drawn from a number of arts but then used this term for other, inappropriate, purposes. Heffernan sees that, since the concept of indeterminacy is common to all the arts called Romantic, the complementary concept of determinacy as used implicitly by Romantic artists requires investigation. His study of Wordsworth, Coleridge, and Turner identifies a Romantic "geometry" capable of representing the infinite and transcendent in artistic and literary media while expressing both limit and form. James Aubrey seeks to define more precisely the meaning and function of the term *picturesque* as Pope uses it, especially for the picturesque garden. Noting the two eighteenth-century senses of *picturesque*—"vividly graphic" and "pleasing to the eye with a variety of light and shade"—he investigates how Pope and Claude Lorrain and Nicholas Poussin combine the two senses in paintings and poems that provide moralizing narratives. Just as Poussin's landscapes draw "both from art and nature everything that is extraordinary in either" to present nature "as we think she ought to be," so Pope becomes both a "Poet in His Landscape" and a "hero in his landscape." Pope views the garden as a heroic landscape, with himself, the moral exemplar, in the foreground.

The theme of the balance of aesthetics and morality that links the problems of defining the Romantic and the picturesque appears in a different form in two following papers which relate more closely works of art and their specific social and historical contexts. Krin Gabbard identifies more clearly the meaning of the Centaur for fifth-century Athenians, showing how the Centaur of the 440s is a different kind of being from that of a generation earlier. Sculptured representations of Centaurs in the 460s present bestial, hubristic creatures with no redeeming social qualities. Centaurs from twenty years later, however, as sculptured on Parthenon friezes or like the Nessus portrayed by Sophocles in the *Trachiniae,* display a range of human qualities, from the bestial and grotesque of the earlier period to those of a newer, pitiable, intellectualized being, a beast seeking but denied full humanity. Gabbard sees this transformation as related to the contemporary Sophists' concern for *sophrosyne,* the human view of the world that seeks to resolve contraries in a natural balance, and as a manifestation of the Athenians' increased interest in the possibilities of their god Dionysus, who personifies and sanctions the irrational and repressed aspects of the human. Dealing with early medieval society, William Cook and Ronald Herzman discuss the climate of tradition and belief that *The Song of Roland* and works of romanesque sculpture share. There is, they think, a common way to interpret both poem and sculptures that allows readers and viewers to understand the works better. They cite in particular the use of Old Testament episodes common to both *Roland* and romanesque church sculpture: for example, Jonah and the King of Nineveh and Daniel in the lions' den prefigure salvation and Christ's resurrection. But even beyond their Christian applications, the Old Testament episodes suggest resonances in the themes and structures of poem and church sculptures as artistic complexes.

In addition to the theme of balance other questions recur throughout this issue, especially how a particular ideology or social viewpoint—or even a criticism of such an ideology—can be expressed in and interpreted from works of varied artistic mediums and forms. Two articles in this issue discuss the relationship between the content of a work of art or literature and the ideology it consciously or unconsciously contains, emphasizing the demands that understanding this relationship places upon the person experiencing the work. Leo Paul de Alvarez discusses the idea of true kingship that pervades Shakespeare's *A Midsummer Night's Dream* and the relationship of this idea to the play's treatment of mimetic action and the creation of images. Throughout his paper, de Alvarez tries to understand the nature of the dream the play is about and of the moon that dominates the action. He sees the question of kingship introduced, in the political context of the wedding of Theseus and Hippolyta, by the question Egeus poses to Theseus about his rights as a father to select his son-in-law. His daughter's choice of the plausible but deceptive Lysander makes him uneasy by challenging his authority. Pursuing the themes of image-making, persuasion, the effects of poetry, and the work of eros, de Alvarez concludes that the traditional constitution of Athens in the play must be supplemented by a dream vision derived from poetry to create among the citizens the true equality Theseus aims at. Lucian Krukowski takes up the question of the difficulty of twelve-tone music for the listener, expanding upon Theodor Adorno's theory about the reason for this difficulty. Adorno had placed the social crises of the early 1900s in the history of music, correlating them by means of a theory that stressed historical discontinuity. Such modern music, he thought, did not develop in an evolutionary manner because it kept reacting to the social matrix of which it was a part and in so doing took the form of social criticism. In contrasting itself with "traditional" music, this modern music made its valuable piece not the "masterwork" but the "radical-work." Starting from this point, Krukowski examines how radical music protests most effectively through the inaccessibility that so plagues its listeners. He argues that twelve-tone music is inaccessible because it is "inaudible," in the sense that there is a radical dissociation of score and performance. Nothing in the score is aimed at direct sensuous appreciation by the listener; the score is determined by intellectual means. This inaudibility that Krukowski describes and the consequent failure of the listener to appreciate the music directly create a sense of deficiency, of a social failure on the listener's part: the music offers a challenge to the way the listener participates in a traditionally structured society and thereby encourages, by its apparent meaninglessness, a replacement of passive acceptance by a perception of new possibilities.

The last two articles pursue further the social and ideological questions introduced in earlier papers. Stephen Smith explains two common misunderstandings of the Marxist Scottish poet Hugh MacDiarmid: the division of his thought into three separate periods to account for its contradictory factors, and the assessment of him as an unorthodox and eccentric Communist. Smith argues that MacDiarmid is best described as a "Scottish Communist," combining Marxism and nationalism in a way that requires understanding three separate elements and their combination. MacDiarmid's Marxism is Leninist, seeing struggles for national emancipation from foreign control as necessary preliminaries to successful class struggles within the freed nations. His economic theories, however, are those of Major C. H. Douglas's social credit system, a form of national capitalism. MacDiarmid ties these two opposing strands together in a theory of a "Caledonian Syzygy," a Celtic commonwealth that, like the Scots themselves, pairs contradictions. MacDiarmid's freed Scotland is to become part of a Gaelic confederation of socialist republics that value the arts which will in turn help to reestablish a balance in world power with the socialist republics of eastern Europe that glorify the all-powerful state. The result will be a means of giving Gaelic artists and workers freedom from constant labor, for pursuing their ethnically inherent aesthetic and intellectual inclinations.

James Kavanagh attempts a similar explanation of the ways an author is misunderstood because of a failure to appreciate the role and nature of ideology in his work. He offers a reading of Melville's "Benito Cereno" that reaches into the meaning of ideology for Americans. Ideology, argues Kavanagh, is something that Americans attempt to present as a façade while they deny the complex of beliefs and practices that really characterizes them by failing or refusing to recognize it as ideology. He posits ideology not as a consciously articulated set of ideas but as a "matrix of presuppositional idea-concepts that construct for one a 'reality' overdetermined by imaginary investments—a formation that resists being made conscious or explicit." "Benito Cereno" is difficult because it becomes a discourse about discourse, embodying the civilized Yankee mind itself as that mind persuades itself that savagery is moral and liberal behavior. Kavanagh describes the means by which Melville achieves this discourse about discourse as the ironic narrative that establishes both Amasa Delano's "lived experience" of and "internal distance" from his ideological "lived relation to the real." Delano's complex sentences force readers either to identify with Delano or to adopt a critical distance from him. The text is often ambiguous; the contradictions it contains reflect those within the author and the reader and help to dissolve the natural sense of self-importance Americans tend to hold.

The editors hope the interconnections in theme and topic among the articles in this issue will stimulate readers to reflect upon their own "lived relations" with the arts, literature, and society.

James M. Heath

BUCKNELL REVIEW

The Arts, Society, Literature

The Arts and Literature

Roland and Romanesque: Biblical Iconography in *The Song of Roland*

William R. Cook
Ronald B. Herzman

State University of New York, Geneseo

THAT there is a useful and fruitful interpenetration between the *Song of Roland* and romanesque art has been noted and documented by such eminent scholars as Erich Auerbach and, more recently, Eugene Vinaver.[1] Readers have learned much about the stylistic milieu of *Roland* from the criticism of these and other scholars, who have taught us to see in the great *chanson de geste* the same solidity, vigor, and forcefulness that form the dominant impression when viewing the stone of the great twelfth-century masons.[2] The dramatic gestures, the comparative flatness of the background, and perhaps most significant, the distortion and abstraction of form that are evident in romanesque art generally and romanesque sculpture in particular provide a most useful analogy with the *Song of Roland,* bringing into high relief the stylistic elements that most separate *Roland* from later fiction, even later medieval fiction. Furthermore, in viewing romanesque art, one is clearly able to perceive the fundamental division between good and evil in the subject matter, the larger-than-life quality of the protagonists, and the hierarchical relationships between characters that are also so important in the composition of *Roland.*

Given the stylistic relationships that have emerged from a perception of a shared climate of thought, it should not be

Figure 1. Right-central tympanum and lintel, cathedral of Angoulême. (All photographs in this chapter are by William R. Cook.)

Figure 2. Detail of Roland lintel, cathedral of Angoulême.

surprising that the connection between *Roland* and romanesque art can be continued beyond such stylistic concerns and extended to similarity in subject matter as well. The presupposition that will guide this paper is that the shared climate of belief and the shared way to articulate that belief which exist in the *Song of Roland* and works of romanesque sculpture—both those having Roland as part of the program and those which depict motifs and stories contained in *Roland*—will allow us to see more clearly the major themes of the poem. Most obviously, Roland is himself the subject of a number of romanesque sculptures.[3] Among the best known of these are the jamb statues on the cathedral of Verona, in which Roland and his companion Oliver, standing opposite each other, flank the main portal.[4] Another famous example, the lintel depicting scenes from the *Song of Roland* on the right central tympanum of the cathedral of Angoulême (figs. 1, 2), is worthy of more extended analysis. Since the lintel is part of a complete sculptural program extending across the entire façade (fig. 3), the Roland tympanum can be analyzed within a larger context, one that can be especially useful when turning from sculpture back to the poem.[5]

The general theme of the five tympana on the façade is the commission of the apostles, a theme that Adolf Katzenellenbogen, in his seminal analysis of the Church of Saint Mary Magdalene in Vézelay, has shown to be intimately connected with the twin themes of crusade and of pilgrimage to Spain, themes that also define the central concerns of *Roland*.[6] The commission of the apostles is itself seen within a larger frame at Angoulême, since an apocalyptic Christ appears on the façade of the cathedral high above the tympana (fig. 4), thus connecting the entire sculptural program with the major romanesque theme of judgment, a connection that also has direct implications for *Roland*—a work that ends in judgment and implies judgment throughout in its depiction of the fundamental struggle between good and evil. The interconnected elements of the program of the Angoulême façade—the commission of the apostles and judgment—are linked thematically as well as spatially: as the precondition of Christ's return in glory (and, as Matthew 24:8 tells us, as a sign of that return as well), it is necessary to spread the Word of Christ throughout the world. The Church Militant prepares the way for the Church Triumphant. In *Roland* too, where the theme of judgment and the

Figure 3. Façade, cathedral of Angoulême.

Figure 4. Apocalyptic Christ, façade, cathedral of Angoulême.

theme of the spread of the faith are both present throughout, the same connection holds true.

A number of details in *Roland* reinforce the thematic connection between the spread of the Christian faith and judgment. Among the most compelling is the time scheme of the poem. It has been pointed out, for example, that the entire action of *Roland* is divided into seven days.[7] The poem is so structured in order to bring the work of Charlemagne into alignment with God's own work in the days of creation; in fighting for the spread of Christianity, Charlemagne suggests by analogy the continuation of God's work in the present.[8] Moreover, these seven days of creation are also analogous to the seven ages of history into which all time is divided, and these two sevens are frequently linked by the church fathers.[9] The seventh age, as Augustine and many others point out, is the age instituted by the return of Christ and the final judgment at the end of time. A subtle reinforcement for looking at the poem in terms of this seven-age scheme is found by recalling that the judgment of Ganelon, the judgment that ends the poem, takes place not only in the seventh day of the poem, but on the feast of St. Sylvester, which not accidentally happens to be 31 December, the last day of the year and thus another reminder of final judgment.

Attention to the specific details of the façade of Angoulême shows that the central tympanum contains Christ flanked by two adoring angels, and that each of the other four tympana contains three apostles, each holding a book. All tympana are surrounded by rich foliage inhabited by both real and mythical animals. The lintels, with the exception of the Roland lintel, also contain foliage and animals. Though most of the apostles are difficult to identify because of a lack of iconographic attributes, Peter with his keys, placed in the tympanum above the Roland lintel (fig. 1), is a significant exception. The upper façade is dominated by Christ in a mandorla surrounded by the four beasts of Revelation 3; to either side are saints in glory and, at a lower level, sinners in punishment. Two military saints are also depicted in the upper façade, George fighting the dragon and Martin with the beggar before the gates of Amiens. These details help reinforce the major thematic concerns of the poem. For example, it is possible to explain the significance of the twelve peers in Roland more fully by suggesting that they are figurally related to the twelve apostles.[10] The connection between *Roland* and Angoulême suggests that apostolic preaching is made present to twelfth-century Christendom by translating it into the language of the crusades. Roland's recitation of his conquests for the faith becomes one more example of the translation of apostolic zeal into crusading fervor.[11] The link between Roland, first among the peers, and Peter, first of the apostles, which is suggested by their relative placement at Angoulême, is also not accidental, for Roland's threefold refusal to blow Olifant parallels Peter's threefold denial, just as his later repentance and redemptive horn-blowing at the climax of the poem are related to Peter's threefold affirmation of love in John 21. The most far-reaching implication of this figural relationship is that the *Song of Roland* is most profitably viewed as a conversion story. Like the Peter of the Gospels, whose characteristic rashness and quickness to anger he shares, Roland must learn though a radical turning of the will. The converted Peter of Acts shows that humility is the necessary precondition to the spreading of the Word that will usher in the Kingdom of God. In his repentance through martyrdom, Roland recreates the same ideal.

The close interrelationship of visual and verbal that is suggested by the thematic connection between the Angoulême Roland and the text of the poem points toward the conclusion that it might well be possible to use thematic parallels in *Roland* and romanesque sculpture to elucidate meaning in *Roland* in even more specific terms. And in fact there are a number of motifs common in romanesque art that find a verbal counterpart in *Roland*. For example, the stylized way in which animals, animal imagery, and foliage are presented in the poem suggests that similar depictions of such animals and plants in romanesque sculpture might tell more about the natural geography of the poem than would simply going to nature itself. A comparison of these two kinds of sources shows the audience that in *Roland*, as in romanesque sculpture, there is no unmediated nature. Both poet and sculptor tend to see nature in the same way, a way that has been described with wonted brilliance by Dom Jean LeClercq:

> Apart from exceptions, they [the monks] do not look at Nature itself to admire it as it is; they see it through literary remembrances coming from the Bible, the Fathers, or classical authors. . . . Nature "in the raw," unembellished by work or art, inspires the learned man with a sort of horror; the abysses and peaks which we like to

Figure 5. Beasts, capital at Chauvigny.

> gaze at, are to him an occasion of fear. . . . In nature, everything is symbolic.[12]

Charlemagne's dream, since it contains such a rich store of animal imagery, can profitably be examined in the light of this view of nature put forth by Father LeClercq:

> With great dismay Charles sees his knights attacked
> By vicious beasts—by leopards and by bears,
> Serpents and vipers, dragons and devils too,
> And there are griffons, thirty thousand and more,
> All of them leaping, charging against the Franks,
> The Franks who cry, "Charlemagne, help us now!"
> And overwhelmed by pity and by grief,
> He starts out toward them, but something interferes:
> A mighty lion springs at him from a wood,
> Fearful to look at, raging and proud and bold.
>
> [ll.2541–50][13]

The conflict described here between Charlemagne's knights and a variety of real and mythical animals clearly is concerned not only with the forthcoming battle with the Moslems but with the larger battle of good versus evil. All the beasts and animals described in the text above can be found representing evil in romanesque sculpture (fig. 5). For example, on the façade of the church at Oloron Ste. Marie there is a lion in the process of devouring a man (fig. 6). In the passage in which Charlemagne commands

> "Let all the dead remain just as they are,
> But keep them safe from lions and wild beasts"
> [ll. 2435–36]

we recognize the symbolic resonances, for the soul must be protected from the forces of evil.

Romanesque art also depicts with some frequency wicked souls being dragged to hell by devils, which is of course also the fate of pagans who die in battle (e. g., ll. 1268 and 1553). Furthermore, as in romanesque art, the animals that appear in the narrative can be either good or bad, depending on the context. The lion that will attack the bodies of the Franks in the passages quoted above obviously represents evil, as do the lions in several Pyrenées churches, including Oloron Ste. Marie, Serrabone, and St. Michel de Cuxa. However, at line 1888 the Franks face their foes like lions—an image of courage and strength that also has its counterpart in romanesque sculpture, for example in the lions supporting the throne of David on the Porte des Comtes at St. Sernin in Toulouse.

While it is true that some of the foregoing motifs are common to *Roland* and romanesque sculpture because they are common to the shared Christian tradition that is the source of both, what we wish to suggest from the above examples is that the artists in both media chose from a very much wider range of possibilities elements from that common tradition which, taken together, suggest that the shared climate of belief may be more precisely described than has previously been noticed. This similarity in ways of seeing prepares the way for an analysis of even more specific connections between *Roland* and romanesque sculpture.

In the prayers of Roland and Charlemagne, several biblical episodes are referred to. Roland's prayer just before he dies contains two biblical references:

> "O my true father, O Thou who never lied,
> Thou who delivered Lazarus from the grave,

Figure 6. Lion eating man, façade, Orlon Ste. Marie.

> Who rescued Daniel out of the lions' den,
> Keep now my soul from every peril safe,
> Forgive the sins that I have done in life."
>
> [ll. 2384–88]

And before Charlemagne fights against the Emir and his army, he offers this prayer:

> "Father in heaven, protect me on this day
> As thou in truth didst rescue Jonah once
> When he was captured and held inside a whale,
> As thou didst spare the King of Nineveh,
> And rescued Daniel from fearful suffering
> When he was thrown inside the lions' den;
> And those three children set in the midst of flames—
> So may Thy love be close to me today!
> And in Thy mercy be gracious to my plea
> That Roland's vengeance may be allowed to me."
>
> [ll. 3100–3109]

An examination of the meaning of these stories mentioned in the two prayers is most useful to understanding *Roland,* and one approach to such an examination is through the representations of these stories in romanesque sculpture.

One point to be made at the outset is that four of the five stories mentioned (Daniel in the lions' den is mentioned twice) are from the Old Testament. Those familiar with romanesque sculpture should not be surprised, since the majority of biblical subjects there are also taken from the Old Testament. For example, in the great church of Mary Magdalene at Vézelay, only four of approximately twenty-seven biblical stories carved on the capitals of the nave come from the New Testament, and none of these depicts Christ. An explanation for the Old Testament-to-New Testament ratio both in *Roland* and the church at Vézelay lies in the religious, and specifically monastic, culture that produced them. This was a culture that stressed the allegorical interpretation of Scripture and loved to express Christian truths under Old Testament figures. Although Christ is not depicted in the nave capitals at Vézelay, men of the Old Testament who prefigured him are prominent, including Adam, Noah, Moses, and David.[14] This love of allegory also explains why the Song of Songs was the biblical book on which the greatest number of commentaries was written in the twelfth century.

It is now worthwhile to turn to the five biblical stories contained in the prayers of Roland and Charlemagne, to their

Figure 7. Raising of Lazarus, capital, cathedral of Vienne.

Figure 8. Women at the tomb of Christ, capital, cathedral of Vienne.

Figure 9. Christ laid in his tomb, capital from cloister, St. Pons (now in the Louvre).

depictions in romanesque sculpture, and to a study of their interpretation in the twelfth century. It is clear from a capital depicting the raising of Lazarus in the cathedral of Vienne (fig. 7) that this event is seen as a prefiguration of Christ's resurrection, since Lazarus's tomb is almost identical to depictions of Christ's tomb both at Vienne and in other romanesque churches (figs. 8,9). Since, according to Paul, all men die with Christ so that they can share his Resurrection, the viewer is meant from looking at Lazarus to call to mind his own resurrection at the last judgment. In the Middle Ages, Lazarus was believed to have been a great sinner who repented before his death, and thus he is also a model of conversion. Clearly, conversion and judgment are also central themes in *Roland*. Furthermore, the Lazarus whom Christ raised was in the Middle Ages identified with the poor man in the parable of Luke 16, and this too is a parable of judgment. Depictions of this parable, for example at Vézelay, show an angel taking the soul of the poor man to heaven, reminiscent of the description of the taking of the soul in Roland after his prayer; the depiction of a demon taking the soul of the rich man of the parable of

Lazarus at Vézelay reminds us of descriptions of demons taking the souls of Moslems killed at Roncesvalles.

According to legends that developed in the eleventh century, Lazarus and his sisters Mary Magdalene and Martha came to France to preach the gospel.[15] Again we recall the importance of the theme of the journey and the spread of the gospel in *Roland.* The relics of Lazarus were venerated at Autun and Avallon. At Autun, the great church of St. Lazarus, now the cathedral, was built as a place of pilgrimage, and acts of repentance were regularly performed outside this great romanesque monument. This shrine of Lazarus is also near the great church dedicated to his sister Mary Magdalene at Vézelay, an important pilgrimage shrine in its own right. But Vézelay was also an important Cluniac house especially related to the crusades; the tympanum in the narthex there is concerned with the spread of the Gospel, and the second and third crusades were in fact begun there. And Vézelay was also the beginning of one of the main pilgrimage routes to Santiago de Compostela in Galicia. Thus Roland's recollections of the raising of Lazarus in his prayer before his death, because of its commonly held associations, recall the important themes of pilgrimage and spread of the Gospel, repentance and conversion, and judgment.

The other biblical event mentioned in Roland's prayer is Daniel's escape from the lions' den. This story is an Old Testament prefiguration of Christ's and also our resurrection, and thus thematically reinforces the story of the raising of Lazarus. The story of Daniel in the lions' den is probably the most frequently depicted story in French romanesque sculpture. In most depictions of the story as related in Daniel 6, the lions are shown as ferocious beasts, suggesting Daniel's danger and the need for God's direct intervention. Other depictions such as that on a capital at Varen show the lions as tamed, and thus suggest Daniel's triumph over death through God's mercy. On the capitals at Vézelay and Saujon (fig. 10), Daniel is shown in a mandorla with the lions unable to penetrate it, the mandorla more clearly identifying Daniel with Christ. However, there is also a somewhat different story of Daniel in the lions' den in the apocryphal Daniel 14, also called "Daniel, Bel, and the Snake." In this version, Daniel is cast into the lions' den for opposing the idolatry associated with Bel and the snake. While in the den, an angel brings the prophet Habakkuk to Daniel to minister to and feed him. This version of the Daniel story is often depicted

Figure 10. Daniel in the lions' den, capital, Saujon.

in romanesque sculpture, for example at Neuilly-en-Donjon, Ste. Radegonde in Poitiers, Autun, and Beaulieu-sur-Dordogne (figs. 11, 12). This form of the story has particular resonances with Roland's prayer just before his death. First, Daniel is not condemned merely for refusing to follow the laws of the Persian king: instead, he has been actively trying to destroy idolatry by showing the fraud of the priests of Bel and the insanity of worshiping a mortal beast. This active struggle against paganism is obviously related to Roland's lifetime mission to bring Christianity to all pagan lands. Furthermore, according to the Daniel 14 story, Daniel stays in the lions' den for six days and is released on the seventh. We recall the seven ages of man, the last of which is the age of judgment. When considered in the light of the seven-day structure of *Roland,* this version of the Daniel story becomes particularly important to a complete understanding of this reference to Daniel in Roland's prayer.[16] Roland shares with Daniel the triumph of the seventh day, which means for Roland the reward of salvation.

The second version of the Daniel story is also relevant to Charlemagne's prayer at Roncesvalles, where the story of the lions' den is also mentioned. Here Charlemagne mentions Daniel as the one whom God rescued from suffering. This seems to be reminiscent of the sending of Habakkuk to Daniel while in the den of lions. Furthermore, Charlemagne is about to do battle with the defenders of idolatry led by the Emir from Babylon, the city where Daniel was thrown into the pit. In his prayer, Charlemagne is calling on God not only to save him from death but also to minister to him in his need just as Habakkuk ministered to Daniel. The common depiction of the Daniel-with-Habakkuk story in romanesque sculpture makes us aware of the importance of the second version of the story, and clearly this story is important for understanding the references to Daniel and the lions' den in the two prayers in *Roland* where the story is mentioned.

Charlemagne also recalls in his prayer the story of the three Hebrews in the fiery furnace, another story from the book of Daniel, in which those in danger are rescued and ministered to by an angel sent from God. And the words of Azariah while in the furnace are remarkably applicable to Charlemagne's situation:

> Grant us again thy marvellous deliverance, and win glory for thy name, O Lord. Let all who do thy servants harm be humbled; may

Figure 11. Daniel in the lions' den ministered by Habakkuk, capital from the façade, Neuilly-en-Donjon.

Figure 12. Daniel in the lions' den ministered by Habukkuk, capital, Ste. Radegonde in Poitiers.

> they be put to shame and stripped of all their power, and may their strength be crushed; let them know that thou alone art the Lord God, and glorious all over the world.
>
> [Dan. 3: 44–45]

This story also has a tradition in the visual arts of the romanesque period, for example on a capital of the church of St. Lazarus in Autun (fig. 13). A careful look at the biblical text referred to in the prayer along with the recognition of a tradition in the visual arts again helps to illuminate the text of *Roland.*

The other two stories recalled in Charlemagne's prayer come from the book of the prophet Jonah. The first is the rescue of Jonah from the belly of the fish, another figure of Christ's resurrection after three days in the tomb; this interpretation of the Jonah story goes back to the Gospels themselves. It is a story associated with pilgrimage and the spread of the word of God, for Jonah has been sent to preach repentance to the Ninevites. This is also a story of Jonah's repentance, since Jonah's misfortunes began because of his unwillingness to respond to God's command to warn the Ninevites. The second reference to Jonah in Charlemagne's prayer concerns God's sparing of the city of Nineveh because its king responds to Jonah's preaching and repents. This story can be linked to Charlemagne's offer to spare the city of Saragossa if its people would repent and heed the commands of God. However, unlike Nineveh, the King of Saragossa is a false penitent through his treachery. Consequently, Charlemagne destroys the city after defeating the Emir just as God would have destroyed Nineveh had its people not heeded His messenger. In a capital at Mozac in the Auvergne, we see the story of Jonah and the fish depicted on one side of a capital, with the gate of Nineveh on the other side (figs. 14, 15). These two incidents are linked together at Mozac for the same reason that they are mentioned together in *Roland.* In Matthew 12 and Luke 11 Christ mentions these two incidents from the book of Jonah in the context of the Jews' lack of faith and their final judgment. Christ tells the Jews that the only sign they will receive will be the sign of Jonah, that is, Christ's own three days in the tomb; then he reminds them that on the day of judgment the men of Nineveh will be present to testify against the Jews and thus secure their damnation. This suggestion of the two Jonah stories linked to the theme of final judgment thus makes them appropriate to the dramatic situa-

Figure 13. The three Hebrews in the fiery furnace, capital, St. Lazarus in Autun.

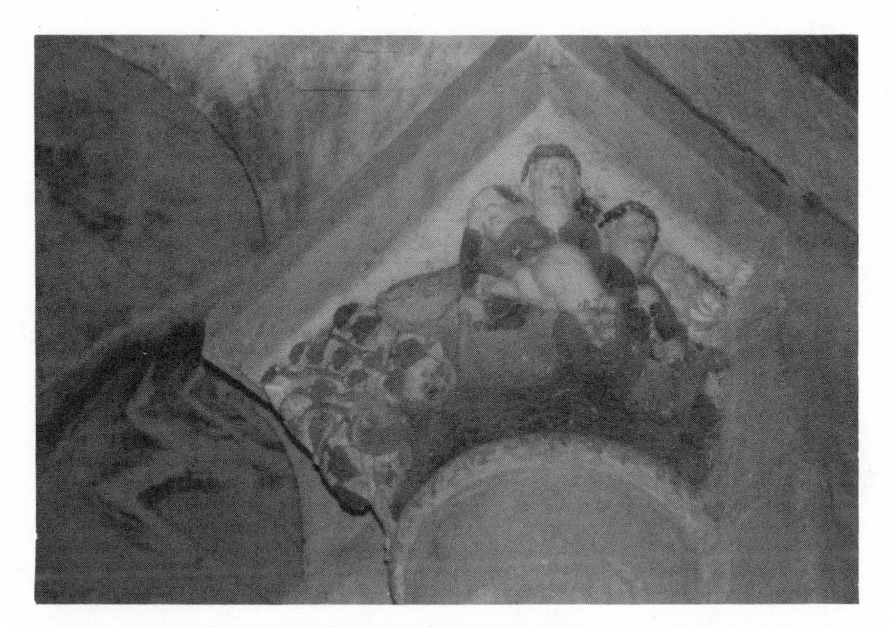

Figure 14. Jonah and the fish, capital, Mozac.

Figure 15. The gate of Nineveh, capital, Mozac.

Figure 16. Left tympanum, Church of St. Peter in Aulnay.

Figure 17. Central portal, Church of St. Peter in Aulnay.

tion in *Roland,* both because of the importance of the theme of judgment to *Roland* generally and because Charlemagne is about to execute judgment for God upon the false Nineveh. And in the two Jonah stories generally, we find the theme of repentance and of the journey to preach the word of God as well as that of judgment.

It is now perhaps possible to carry even farther the presupposition that has guided the paper thus far, of a shared climate of belief and a shared way to articulate that belief, by comparing *Roland* to the sculptural program of a romanesque façade in which there is no specific depiction of either Roland or the biblical stories mentioned in the poem. Even here the concerns of the designer of the façade and the author of *Roland* are so close that the word and stone reinforce each other. Such a program can be found on the façade of the church of St. Peter at Aulnay in the Saintonge. The left and right tympana contain respectively the crucifixion of St. Peter and the glorification of Peter and another saint with Christ between them. Each tympanum is surrounded by richly carved foliage. The central portal has no tympanum but has four richly carved archivolts (figs. 16, 17, 18). The innermost contains angels with the Lamb of God; the second depicts the triumph of the virtues over the vices taken directly from the *Psychomachia* of Prudentius (figs. 19, 20).[17] In the third are the wise and foolish virgins from the parable in Matthew 25, and in the outer archivolt are the signs of the zodiac and the works of the months. The two tympana suggest the final victory through martyrdom of Peter, who denied Christ three times but repented and spread the word of God abroad and finally died for the faith. There is, as we have said, a clear analogy between this and the victory of Roland, whose triple act of pride in refusing to blow Olifant was followed by repentance and martyrdom while spreading the word of God. The lush foliage of the archivolts around the two Peter tympana is reminiscent of the descriptions in *Roland* of the lush foliage of paradise (ll. 2197, 2898–99).

By reading the archivolts of the central portal from the outermost inwards, we learn first from the calendar that what is presented here occurs within time, traditionally the time between the first and second comings of Christ.[18] From the next archivolt, concerning the wise and foolish virgins, we learn that what exists in time will be subjected to a judgment for eternity.[19] The archivolt depicting the struggle of the virtues and the vices

Figure 18. Right tympanum, Church of St. Peter in Aulnay.

Figure 19. Faith and Idolatry, central portal archivolt, Aulnay.

Figure 20. Concord and Discord, central portal archivolt, Aulnay.

from Prudentius suggests that what occurs on earth before the judgment is an all-out struggle between good and evil; the side that one takes in this struggle will determine one's fate at the judgment. The angels with the Lamb of God in the last archivolt offer a promise of repose with Christ for those who choose to fight for him. The concerns of the designer of this sculptural program are remarkably similar to those of the author of *Roland.* The temporal framework of Roland has already been discussed, and it is emphasized by the Joshua-like miracle of stopping the sun when Charlemagne returns to Roncesvalles (l. 2460). The recognition that man's actions will be submitted to a judgment which will stand for eternity is also a central concern of *Roland,* as stressed continuously by Turpin in his short battlefield sermons (e.g., ll. 1522–23) and the references to St. Michael, the angel associated with final judgment according to the book of Daniel and in romanesque sculpture. That *Roland* is a story of an all-out struggle between good and evil is evident from all that has been discussed above. The descriptions of the Moslems compared to those of Christian warriors recall the descriptions in and depictions of the *Psychomachia* of

Prudentius. Finally, Roland's soul being borne to paradise reminds us that those who fight for God's truth in this life will receive their reward in eternity.

Contemporaneous works such as the *Song of Roland* and French romanesque sculpture share certain stylistic and iconographic similarities. In addition, they share a way of making the truths contained in Scripture relevant to the problems of their own day. They present a common way of "translating" the eternal truths of the Bible into a course of action for a society quite different from the one in which they were written. In particular, in these works we are shown how the truths of the Bible were to be lived out in an age of struggle between Cross and Crescent, how Christ's command to preach the Gospel to the ends of the earth was to be fulfilled, how men could prepare the way for the second coming of Christ and the final judgment. An examination of *Roland* and romanesque together leads us toward a fuller understanding of both because certain elements of thought and meaning can be more fully detected in one medium than in another and then tested to see whether they do in fact pertain to the other as well.

Notes

1. Erich Auerbach, *Mimesis: The Representation of Reality in Western Literature,* trans. Willard R. Trask (Princeton, N.J.: Princeton University Press, 1953), chap. 5, "Roland and Ganelon"; Eugene Vinaver, *The Rise of Romance* (Oxford: Oxford University Press, 1971), chap. 1.

2. A more complete list of works that examine the relationship between *Roland* and romanesque style would include the following: Fern Farnham, "Romanesque Design and the *Chanson de Roland,*" *Romance Philology* 18 (1964–65): 143–64; Guy R. Mermier, "More About Unity in the *Song of Roland,*" Olifant 2 (1974–75): 91–108; Charles R. Dodwell, "The Bayeux Tapestry and the French Secular Epic," *The Burlington Magazine* 108 (1966): 549–60; Ronald B. Herzman and M. Kay Nellis, "The Gateway of Art: Analogies as an Approach to Medieval Literature," *Exercise Exchange* 17 (1973): 13–17. See also the iconographic analysis in Gerald Brault, *The Song of Roland: An Analytical Edition* (University Park, Pa: The Pennsylvania State University Press, 1978), vol. 1 (Introduction and Commentary).

3. These have been documented in great detail in Rita Lejeune and Jacques Stiennon, *The Legend of Roland in the Middle Ages,* trans. Christine Trollope (New York: Phaidon Books, 1971). This valuable work is an attempt at a complete documentation of Roland in the art of the Middle Ages.

4. See Rita Lejeune, "Roland et Olivier au portail du Dôme de Vérone," *Cultura Neolatina* 22 (1961): 229–45.

5. The problem of identification of the scenes has been effectively dealt with by Rita

Lejeune. See "Le Linteau d'Angoulême et *La Chanson de Roland,*" *Romania* 82 (1961): 1–26, esp. pp. 11 ff.

6. Adolf Katzenellenbogen, "The Central Tympanum at Vézelay, Its Encyclopedic Meaning and Its Relation to the First Crusade," *Art Bulletin* 26 (1944): 141–51.

7. See Robert A. Kunkle, "Time in the *Song of Roland,*" *Romance Notes* 13 (1971–72): 550–55.

8. The figure of Charlemagne as emperor has strong associations with the last days and with judgment. The prophecy of a Last World Emperor, who comes at the end of the sixth age, converts pagans, defeats opponents of Christianity, and then ushers in doomsday, was often associated with a French tradition of a Second Charlemagne. Moreover, interest in these prophecies was heightened at the time of the First Crusade. The figure of the Last World Emperor has been extensively documented by Marjorie Reeves, *The Influence of Prophecy in the Later Middle Ages: A Study in Joachimism* (London: Oxford University Press, 1969). See pp. 301–2 and passim. See also Norman Cohn, *The Pursuit of the Millennium* (New York: Oxford University Press, 1970). Texts connected with the Last World Emperor have been edited by Ernst Sackur, *Sibyllinische Texte und Forschungen* (Halle: Max Niemeyer, 1898). These include the so-called Tiburtine Sibyl, Adso's *Life of Antichrist,* and Pseudo-Methodius.

9. For the correspondence between the days of creation and the ages of time as understood by the fathers, see Auguste Luneau, *L'Histoire du salut chez les Pères de l'Eglise: la doctrine des ages du monde* (Paris: Beauchesne, 1964), and Jean Daniélou, *The Bible and the Liturgy* (Notre Dame, Ind.: University of Notre Dame Press, 1956), esp. chaps. 14, 15, and 16. Standard sources of this correspondence include Isidore of Seville, *Etymologiae* (*Patrologia Latina* 82: 224–28); Bede, *In Principium Genesis* (*Corpus Christianorum Series Latina* 118A: 1–39); Bede, *De sex dierum creatione* (*Patrologia Latina* 93: 219); Bede, *De temporum ratione* (*Patrologia Latina* 90: 520–71). Among the many references to this subject in Augustine is this passage from the *City of God:* "Now if the epochs of history are reckoned as 'days,' following the apparent temporal scheme of Scripture, this Sabbath period will emerge more clearly as the seventh of these epochs. . . . After this present age God will rest, as it were, on the seventh day, and He will cause us, who are the seventh day, to find our rest in Him." *Concerning the City of God Against the Pagans,* trans. Henry Bettenson (Baltimore, Md.: Penguin Books, 1972), p. 1091. A complete discussion of all the varied correspondences connected with the days of creation can also be found in St. Bonaventure's *Collationes in Hexaemeron* (Quaracchi, 5. 327–454). An English translation of this work can be found in *The Works of Bonaventure,* vol. 5, trans. José de Vinck (Patterson, N.J.: St. Anthony Guild Press, 1970). Although the work postdates *Roland,* it is, in good scholastic fashion, a veritable encyclopedia of scriptural and Patristic sources on the Hexameral tradition.

10. See June Hall Martin, "The Divisions of the *Chanson de Roland,*" *Romance Notes* 6 (1964–65): 182–95.

11. Cohn has pointed out (chap. 3) how the expectation of a millennial kingdom was connected with crusading fervor.

12. Jean LeClercq, *The Love of Learning and the Desire for God,* trans. Catherine Misrahi (New York: Fordham University Press, 1961), pp. 164–65.

13. Quotations are from the translation of Patricia Terry (Indianapolis, Ind: Bobbs-Merrill, 1965).

14. Adam, Noah, Moses, and David are also key Old Testament figures in the division of history into seven ages, each the representative of a different age. It is also worth pointing out that this love for figural interpretation of the Old Testament pro-

vides a support for the figural interpretation suggested by the structure of *Roland.* The same delight in seeing truth under figure is present in both.

15. The main outlines of the development of the Mary Magdalene story, of such importance in monastic writings in the eleventh and twelfth centuries, can be found in Helen Meredith Garth, *Saint Mary Magdalene in Mediaeval Literature,* Johns Hopkins University Studies in Historical and Political Science, Ser. 67, no. 3 (Baltimore, Md.: Johns Hopkins University Press, 1950). See also Victor Saxer, *Le Culte de Marie Madeleine en occident, des origines à la fin du moyen âge* (Paris: Clavreuil, 1959).

16. The connection between Daniel and Judgment is supported by the tradition of Jerome's Commentary on the Book of Daniel and commentaries on the Apocalypse placed together in the same manuscript. As Emile Mâle tells us, in referring to the St.-Sever Apocalypse: "The manuscript does not end with the Beatus commentary on the Book of Revelation, but with a treatise by St. Jerome on the interpretation of the Book of Daniel. There are, in fact, singular analogies between the visions of St. John and of Daniel, which explain their juxtaposition. Both the Old and the New Testaments prophesy, with the same air of mystery, the reign of the Beast at the end of time; the same sense of terror emanates from both books." *Religious Art in France, The Twelfth Century: A Study of the Origins of Medieval Iconography,* ed. Harry Bober and trans. Marthiel Mathews, Bollingen Series 90 (Princeton, N.J.: Princeton University Press, 1978), pp. 8–10. Jerome's Commentary on Daniel was the most important exegesis of the work in the Middle Ages.

17. A connection betwen *Roland* and Prudentius has been noted by Emmanuel J. Mickel, Jr., in "Parallels in Prudentius' *Psychomachia* and *La Chanson de Roland,*" *Studies in Philology* 67 (1970): 439–52.

18. An example of this use of the signs of the zodiac in Gothic sculpture occurs at the cathedral of Amiens. The left portal of the façade is concerned with the church militant, which exists from the time of Christ's coming (represented on the right portal) to the time of Christ's return in glory to judge the living and the dead (the central portal). The quatrefoils under the jamb statues on the left portal contain the signs of the zodiac and the works of the months, ways of measuring the time between the first and the second comings of christ.

19. That the wise and foolish virgins are usually understood as a symbol of the end of time and as a sign of the second coming can be seen in a literary example, the so-called *Sponsus* play from St. Martial at Limoges, which has been edited by Karl Young in *The Drama of the Medieval Church,* 2 vols. (Oxford: Clarendon Press, 1933), 2: 361–69. The scheme on the façade at Aulnay can be seen temporally as follows: the zodiac, present time, sixth age; the virgins, future time, end of the sixth age; judgment, future time, division between sixth and seventh ages; rest, future time, the seventh age.

Wordsworth, Coleridge, and Turner: The Geometry of the Infinite

James A. W. Heffernan

Dartmouth College

IT will probably never be possible to formulate an adequate definition of *romantic*. Yet if the word is indefinable, it is likewise indispensable. We use it not only to categorize the music, literature, and visual arts of the later eighteenth and earlier nineteenth centuries, but also to justify—implicitly or explicitly—the growing number of recent studies that compare the arts of this period with each other. Presently fashionable but often suspected—and sometimes justly accused—of lacking scholarly rigor, comparisons of the arts now seem more than ever in need of period rubrics to contain them, for as Alastair Fowler has noted, "the notion of a universally valid systematic correspondence between the arts must be regarded as a chimera."[1]

If we turn from this chimera to the notion of a correspondence among the arts of a particular period, we seem to stand on firmer ground. In fact we continue to stand on our own assumptions, or more precisely on the two assumptions that Meyer Schapiro finds beneath all approaches to the history of culture: "that every style is peculiar to a period of culture and that, in a given culture or epoch of culture, there is only one style or a limited range of styles."[2] How is this style or range of styles discovered? In theory, it arises from the perception of specific correspondences between or among the arts of a given period. "Our existing period concepts," says Fowler, "have all been arrived at in the light of interart analogies, on whose validity their own depends" ("Periodization," p. 488). This statement is highly problematic. Period concepts may well derive from interart analogies, just as governments—including monarchies—may ultimately derive from social contracts. But to explain the genesis of a concept is not to account for the way we use it, or for the fact that we use it at all. If A. O. Lovejoy's well-known dissection of "Romanticism" has failed to make us relinquish the notion that it has a coherent meaning or at least a coherent set of meanings, would we be moved to relinquish this notion by any amount of evidence about the disparity between Wordsworth and Constable, or Goethe and Beethoven, or Schiller and Casper David Friedrich? Whether or not period concepts originate from interart analogies, such concepts eventually assume an independent and indestructible life of their own. By turns validating and being validated by specific comparisons, they keep the historian of culture in a hermeneutic circle writ large.

To break out of the circle that so often surrounds discussions of Romantic poetry and painting, I propose in this essay to reconsider one of the most conspicuous means by which the arts called "Romantic" are commonly linked—namely, the concept of indeterminacy. To look at this concept critically is to see the need for a complementary concept of determinacy, for a new understanding of what specific poets and painters did with line and geometrical form.

I

The association of the Romantic with the indeterminate is at least as old as A. W. Schlegel's distinction between Romantic and Classic. In Hazlitt's account of this distinction, published in 1816, the Classic style normally "describes things as they are interesting in themselves" while the Romantic style describes them "for the sake of the association of ideas connected with them. . . . The one is the poetry of form, the other of effect."[3] Significantly, Schlegel's distinction cuts across one of the lines that Augustan critics drew between the visual and verbal arts. While Augustan critics thought that suggestiveness was the province of the verbal arts and that the visual arts should deal in determinate forms, Schlegel presumes that poetry and the visual arts are both capable of being either explicit or suggestive. He connects Classic poetry with the imitative precision of Greek sculpture, and Romantic poetry (what Hazlitt calls the poetry of "the moderns") with the chromatic and chiaroscuric effects of painting.[4] But of course we do not now need Schlegel to help us categorize Romantic painting. We can turn instead to Wolfflin's distinction between the linear style of painting, which stresses clear, sharp-edged forms, and the *malerisch* or painterly style, which "blurs the limits, contours, and boundaries of visual or plastic forms."[5]

Romantic painting seems to fit easily into the *malerisch* category, and thus readily lends itself to comparison with Romantic poetry. Both can be seen as manifestations of that Romantic indeterminacy wherein atmosphere dissolves form. It was for "spreading the tone, the *atmosphere* . . . of the ideal world" over natural objects that Coleridge saluted Wordsworth in the *Biographia Literaria,* and in 1816, just about the time that book was published, Hazlitt made a similar though less flatteringly intended comment about Turner, whose pictures he thought were "too much abstractions of aerial perspective, and representations not properly of the objects of nature as of the medium through which they were seen."[6] Wordsworth himself compared his own style to that of Rembrandt, who was Turner's idol; in the transforming effect of Rembrandt's chiaroscuro he reportedly saw "an analogy to his own mode of investing the minute details of nature with an atmosphere of sentiment" (*CWH,* 11: 93). And as for Turner himself, in response to a buyer who was bothered by his indistinctness, he is long supposed to have said, "Indistinctness is my forte."[7]

A recent study of the source of this statement informs us that Turner actually said "fault."[8] But it will take more than a correction of that kind to make us see the inadequacy of a formula that would reduce the English Romantic vision of landscape to a revolution of atmosphere against line, and specifically against the "firm and determined outline" recommended by Joshua Reynolds, who said that painters should know and precisely express "the exact form which every part of nature ought to have" (*D,* p. 52). The apparently simple antithesis between Augustan form and Romantic atmosphere gets complicated as soon as we look at it closely. If Reynolds thought a firm outline indispensable to the portrayal of the human figure, he also thought that "no correctness of form is required" in the rendering of things such as clouds (*D*, p. 223). Only in the Romantic period—and specifically in the work of Constable—do we find systematic studies of cloud formations.

Constable's interest in the shapes of clouds is just one manifestation of the way in which a consciousness of line decisively informs the English Romantic vision of landscape. Students of Blake have long recognized that his figurally based art is conspicuously linear. What I wish to argue here—using Wordsworth, Coleridge, and Turner as the chief examples—is that the Romantic vision of landscape has a linearity of its own, that Romantic poets and painters studied the lines of landscape just as carefully as they studied its atmospheric effects. In fact, precisely because they wished to capture the ever changing life of a landscape in motion, they had to know more about form than their Augustan predecessors did—not less. To represent the indeterminacy of landscape, and at the same time to externalize their own consciousness of infinity, they had to measure what they felt to be measureless. In essence, they had to formulate a geometry of the infinite.

II

The geometry of the infinite begins on the boundaries of the finite. Wordsworth defined the experience of sublimity as a consciousness of "immeasurable" power, and the kind of poetry that moved him most, he said once, was the poetry of "infinity . . . where things are lost in each other, and limits vanish."[9] Yet Wordsworth knew only too well that in order to express this feeling of limitlessness, the poet had to establish—implicitly or explicitly—the limits he was crossing. In the account of his boyhood that appears in Book 1 of *The Prelude*, Wordsworth writes that a huge cliff seemed to rise up over him one evening as he rowed across a lake in a stolen boat. Towering between him and the stars, the cliff seems to cross the line between earth and sky, animate and inanimate, nature and supernature. The line is crossed, however, only after it has been decisively drawn. Before the cliff emerges at all, the boy has "fix'd" his gaze upon an object equally fixed: the summit of a ridge, which forms "the bound of the horizon." With a painter's sense of spatial definition, Wordsworth thus establishes the most important line in his landscape, and at the very moment when the cliff emerges we are made to see this line again:

> When from behind that craggy Steep, till then
> The bound of the horizon, a huge Cliff,
> As if with voluntary power instinct,
> Uprear'd its head.
>
> [l. 405–9][10]

Till then / The bound of the horizon: The sublime sense of awe and terror communicated by the passage as a whole begins at this moment, when the line that had *till then* been the horizon is crossed, and the new horizon, no longer fixed, rises upward to infinity.

Wordsworth's vision of an uncontrollably rising horizon is paradigmatically Romantic. Tolerating neither absolute limit nor absolute division, the Romantic poets characteristically tend to unbind or dissolve the most fundamental line in the landscape. Their horizons ascend toward the limitless height of the sky or into the limitless obscurity of its atmosphere. In Wordsworth's description of the Simplon Pass, the height of the decaying woods is "immeasurable" and the torrents seem to shoot down "from the clear blue sky" (*Prelude* 6: 556, 561). When the sky is clouded, the line between the earth and sky may be dissolved by mist as well as lifted to infinity. On a walking tour of Scotland in 1803, Coleridge saw a waterfall whose summit "appeared to blend with the sky and clouds," and, as he later reported, he considered it "in the strictest sense of the word, a sublime object" (*BL,* 2: 224–25, 308).

For Wordsworth and Coleridge, then, sublimity is a consciousness of *boundaries crossed.* But both words must be italicized. Without consciousness of a boundary, there is no consciousness of crossing, transcendence, or infinity. Even the boundless immensity of the sky must be seen through the framework of a bounded form—as Coleridge reveals in this description of the sky over Malta in 1804:

> O that Sky, that soft blue mighty Arch, resting on the mountains or solid Sea-like plain / what an aweful adorable omneity in unity. I know no other perfect union of the sublime with the beautiful, that is, so that they should both be felt at the same moment tho' by different faculties yet each faculty predisposed by itself to receive the specific modification from the other. To the eye it is an inverted Goblet, the inside of a sapphire Bason; = it is immensity, but even the eye feels as it were to look *thro'* with dim sense of the non resistence / it is not exactly the feeling given to the organ by solid & limited things / the eye itself feels that the limitation is in its own power not in the Object.[11]

Like the vault of paved heaven to which the materialistic singer of Blake's "Mad Song" drives his desperate notes, the sky first seems a finite hemispherical closure: an arch, an inverted goblet, or an inverted basin. When the doors of perception are cleansed, when the eye of the mind makes the eye of the body see beyond the limits of its purely physical powers, the dome of the universe unresistingly dissolves, and the sky becomes a thing of limitless immensity. But Coleridge does not take the Blakean leap from one kind of perception to the other. Even though his eye may feel that it is gazing on infinity, it continues also to feel the sense of enclosure, for the sky gives him "at the same moment," he says, the beauty of the finite and the sublimity of the infinite. What Coleridge reveals to us here is that for him the experience of limitlessness presupposes the consciousness of limit.

He had touched on this paradox two years earlier in "Hymn Before Sunrise," where the night sky is first envisioned as a "substantial" mass of blackness which "thou [Mont Blanc] piercest," and then as the mountain's enclosure: "thy crystal shrine, / Thy habitation from eternity!" (ll. 9–12). In Shelley's "Mont Blanc," of 1816, which echoes the "Hymn," the peak once again "pierc[es] the infinite sky" (l. 60), but this time the sky is both explicitly infinite and finite enough to *be* pierced. Shelley's consciousness of finite form in this poem continually participates in his vision of infinitude. In section 4, the river of ice that flows from the peak of the mountain descends from "the boundaries of the sky"; in the final section, the sky is oxymoronically called "the infinite dome / Of Heaven" (ll. 140–41). Like Coleridge at Malta, Shelley sees the limitlessness of the sky through the limits of a determinate form.

The pictorial counterpart of this determinate indeterminacy is provided by Turner. In the course of lectures that he initiated in 1811 as Professor of Perspective at the Royal Academy, he strongly emphasized "the principles of Lines."[12] But he also said that lines were powerless to represent certain effects, that linear perspective had sometimes to be supplanted by "Aerial Perspective," which involved "the aid of shadow, reduced light, and weaker tones of color." (TMS M f.22–24). In aerial perspective, lines become zones of gradation, and by these zones Turner defines what is indefinable by outlines.

I will take as a case in point a painting from Turner's last and most "atmospheric" decade—*Yacht Approaching the Coast,* painted circa 1840–45 (fig. 1). In this picture the setting sun fills the center of the sky with a distinguishable cone of soft white light. In fact, as Lawrence Gowing has shown, pictures like this one actually defy the principle of "picturesque" asymmetry, the doctrine that light "should never be placed so as to form a line" (*TIR,* p. 27). Yet it is hardly possible to trace the outline of the cone in Turner's sky. We can apprehend the cone, but we cannot see precisely where it begins and ends. Its borders are intangibly aerial, and even as we study its shape, its outline seems to dissolve beneath our eyes.

Correspondingly, the horizon in this picture is at once established and elusive. The left and right sides of the sea in the foreground are decisively darker than the sky, and the short row of buildings in the background at left begins to mark the line between the two elements. But across the rest of the picture no line can be seen. Turning pale in the distance, the sea dissolves into the still paler sky, and the continuity between them is

Figure 1. Turner, *Yacht Approaching the Coast.* (The Tate Gallery, London. Reprinted by permission.)

enhanced by the setting sun, which fills the middle of each with corresponding cones of light. Nevertheless, the hourglass of light thus formed is bisected by the implied horizon, and the pale green wave-textured light of the cone in the sea subtly distinguishes it from the whiter, aerial light of the cone in the sky. The very thing that enhances the continuity between the sea and the sky thus helps also to differentiate them, to reenforce the implied horizon, and to create a series of triangles radiating from the center of the picture. The triangles are not outlined, but they are unmistakably there, for the geometrical structure of this picture is as powerful as it is indeterminate.

Significantly, the yacht in this picture seems to be floating in the air as well as on the water. Neither bound to visible masts nor visibly attached to the speckled red blot of a hull beneath them, its crisply defined sails are three white crescents hovering a space—a piece of visual synecdoche. They call to mind the fleet of ships to which Milton compares the flying Satan in Book 2 of *Paradise Lost:* the fleet which, seen from a distance, "Hangs in the clouds" (ll. 636–37). Because it thus transcends the horizontal boundary between the sea and sky, Wordsworth found this Miltonic fleet sublime. Its "track, we know and feel, is upon the waters" he wrote, "but, taking advantage of its appearance to the senses, the Poet dares to represent it as *hanging in the clouds,* both for the gratification of the mind in contemplating the image itself, and in reference to the motion and appearance of the sublime object to which it is compared" (*PrW,* 3: 31). Wordsworth's comment might well apply to Turner's picture. Like Milton's fleet, Turner's yacht seems to hover in space, at once supported by water and suspended in air. It occupies that indeterminate zone in which the sea virtually *becomes* the sky.

But Turner's yacht has a further analogue in the poetry of Coleridge. At the beginning of part 3 of "The Rime," the spectre bark appears in the distance as "a something *in the sky*" (emphasis mine). Successively appearing as a little speck, a mist, and then "a certain shape," its indeterminacy of form is reenforced by its indeterminacy of position, or more precisely, by the illusion that it is moving through the sky rather than on the sea. When it is near enough to be recognized and joyously hailed as "a sail! a sail!" (here the synecdoche is verbal as well as visual), it is definitely on the sea, cleaving the water "with upright keel." But Coleridge's description of the way the sun descends behind this mysterious craft at once acknowledges the horizon and transcends it:

> The western wave was all a-flame.
> The day was well nigh done!
> Almost upon the western wave
> Rested the broad bright Sun;
> When that strange shape drove suddenly
> Betwixt us and the Sun.
>
> [ll. 171–76]

Like the yacht in Turner's picture, the spectre bark appears in the distance with the setting sun behind it. Against a sky that is almost certainly cloudless, the mariner sees the edge of the western wave, for he is able to tell us precisely that the sun rests "almost" upon it. But he also sees the western wave as "all a-flame," the distant sea turned into fire by the sun's reflected light. As it drops, the setting sun burns through the horizon, and when the spectre bark passes in front of the sun, the mariner sees no horizontal boundary between earth and sky: only the vertical "bars" and sails of the ship glancing "in the sun." After "the Sun's rim dips" and "the stars rush out," the horizon is implicitly reestablished, but when Coleridge tells us that the spectre bark shoots off "o'er the sea," he is once again describing a craft that may be moving *on* the sea or *above* it, in the sky. Like Turner and like Milton too, Coleridge exploits the naturally ambiguous appearance of a distant ship. And fittingly, this ambiguous thing of sea and space makes its appearance in a world where the horizon is at once acknowledged and transcended, where the sea and the sky become halves of a continuous whole, where the water burns as relentlessly as the sky above it, and where—as the mariner says in part 4—"the sky and the sea, and the sea and sky / Lay like a load on my weary eye" (ll. 250–51).

Chiastically interchangeable, the sea and the sky of Coleridge's "Rime" help to reenforce the consciousness of crossing expressed by the poem as a whole, which takes us from the "real" world of the wedding to the fantastic world of spectres and spirits, from the depths of the sea to the middle and upper air, from the visible to the invisible, from the stormy South Pole to the becalmed Pacific, from life to death and back again. Slain by the mariner's crossbow—or, so to speak, crucified on it—the albatross is hung about the mariner's neck "instead of the cross," but the poem is full of crossings, and they significantly include the crossing of the equatorial line. Coleridge establishes lines precisely in order to cross them. Like Wordsworth and Turner, he implicitly reminds us that the very word *infinite* contains and presupposes the finite.

III

This dialectical relation between the finite and the infinite changes subtly but significantly when we turn from lines to geometrical forms. Geometry offered more than a line to be crossed en route to the infinite; it offered forms of immaterial and hence transcendent permanence. The Euclidean stone that appears in Book 5 of *The Prelude* signifies "a bond / Of reason, undisturbed by space or time" (1850 *Prelude* 5: 104–5), and Turner uses similar words at the end of his first Royal Academy lecture, where he quotes from Akenside's *Pleasures of the Imagination:*

> Peculiar in the realms of Space or Time
> Such is the throne which man for truth amid
> The paths of mutability hath built
> Secure unshaken, still; and whence he views,
> In matters mouldering structures, the pure forms
> Of Triangle, or Circle, Cube, or Cone.[13]

Akenside draws, I think, on the traditional assumption that thrones and architectural structures—whether mouldering or not—can be seen as embodiments of pure geometrical forms. But when Turner quotes these lines, he is thinking not so much of architecture as of landscape, and of his own life-long struggle to elicit pure geometrical forms from an atmosphere in motion. Fascinated with mist and rainbows, he captures such evanescent things only by perpetuating the outlines that they momentarily assume or imply, by preserving the very moment at which those fleeting shapes approximate permanent geometrical figures, undisturbed by space or time. In *Buttermere Lake,* for instance, exhibited in 1798, a rainbow and its reflection together compose an arc of light and thus suggest the permanence of the completed circle.

Nevertheless, geometry never becomes the instrument by which Romantic poets and painters categorically "organized" the landscape. In Romantic poetry and painting, the solid arch of architecture gives way to the liquid arch of the waterfall, the aerial arch of the rainbow, the ever shifting rondure of clouds. Such things cannot be simply frozen into circles. And even in relatively fixed and solid forms such as trees, painters and poets conscious of geometrical figures found shapes which at once suggested those figures and yet defied their control. To represent such forms, they had to portray the vital interaction of angle and curve.

Their concept of geometrical interaction may be instructively compared with eighteenth-century theories of geometrical decorum. In *The Analysis of Beauty* (1753), Hogarth said that beauty springs from undulation, a line of tempered variety free of any fixed geometrical form and uninterrupted by sharp turns. Straight lines, circles, and angular forms were in Hogarth's opinion ridiculous.[14] The *Analysis* was shortly followed by Edmund Burke's *Sublime and Beautiful* (1757), which treated straight lines and angles as marks of the sublime, and which therefore made an aesthetic place for angularity. But like Hogarth, Burke thought curvature a mark of beauty, and his distinction between the sublime and the beautiful is based—in part—on the opposition between angles and curves (*SB*, pp. 155–56). After Burke the opposition was restated by Reynolds, who believed that a painter had to choose between "sublime" or energetic angularity and "elegant" or reposeful curvature (*D*, pp. 78–79, 237–38).

Turner refused to make this choice. In his very first lecture he said that painting could express motion "only . . . by an appearance of action, *in opposition to that of repose;* this is the necessity of the triangle" (TMS K f.7^{v}; emphasis mine). For Turner's eye the triangle implies intersection, and as he goes on to say in an 1818 revision of the first lecture, an intersection suggests the radius of a circle, a line of power centrifugally thrusting outward. "As the laws of [motion *commence* / action proceed] from the *radius* of a *circle,* as the periphera of a wheel, so the rotatory power of the joints of the Human Figure, are deductable, and that *action* continues . . . in *straight lines,* as the power of action proceeds, as the flow produced by the arm increases in force [as] the bone[s] of the forearm and Bracchia approach a straight line" (TMS S f.12).

Turner's own work abundantly illustrates the kind of energy that springs from the interaction of angle and curve, of circle

Figure 2. Turner, *Calais Pier, with French Poissards Preparing for Sea: An English Packet Arriving*. (The National Gallery, London. Reprinted by permission.)

and radial line. In *Calais Pier*, first exhibited in 1803 (fig. 2), the churning white frenzy of the sea is embraced by the long curving arm of the pier: a curve repeated in the clouds overhead, in the outer edge of the white sail at the center, and in the shallow trough of the waves in the foreground. Contraposed to all of these curves are the rectilinear masts of the heaving boats, especially of the two in the middle that lean to the right, radically cutting the curve of the pier as well as the curving masses of cloud. Yet Turner does more than juxtapose curves and straight lines; he integrates them. The diagonal sides of the pier at the lower right sharply converge as they recede from the eye, and then become part of a distant curve. Contrastingly, the sails of the boat to the left of center are elegantly curved, but the line of their curves flows into the basically rectilinear mast, and the line of beauty thus becomes a spine of power.

The dynamic cooperation of curves, angles, and straight lines in the external world is something that repeatedly caught the attention of Coleridge. His notebooks show that he found geometrical forms almost everywhere in nature.[15] But what truly fascinated him was the vital interaction of those forms, the way in which natural objects eluded the control of any one geometrical figure. The perfect symmetry of rectilinear forms struck him as lifeless. In a notebook entry of 1802, he objected to a garden with "tyrannically strait parallelogram enclosures," and later he said that nature herself has no perfectly straight lines, but lines *animated* by the curve, the emblem of motion, spontaneity, and inner life.[16] The square and the circle, he observed, can be infinitely combined for pleasure (*NC,* 2: 2342), and in Coleridge's experience of landscape such geometrical impossibilities as the squared circle, the angular curve, and the curved straight line became not merely possibilities but facts. He once noted a piece of land "imperceptibly declin[ing] from horizontal into slope": he noted the combination of curve and straight line in a waterfall; and he more than once observed that a mountain could form what he called "a spherical triangle."[17] In "Hymn Before Sunrise," in fact, Mont Blanc appears both angular and spherical, a piercing "wedge" of "sky-pointing peaks" that nonetheless rises "like a vapoury cloud" (ll. 9–10, 70–80).

He was equally struck with the geometrical complexity of ships. In a notebook entry of 1804, he observed that the determinate outline of wind-swollen sails makes them a combination of straight edge and curve (*NC,* 1: 2012 f.39). And shortly afterwards, he reflected on the geometrical complexity of ships as a whole—in words that might readily apply to the vessels in *Calais Pier:*

> Ships, & their Picturesqueness—/Have I noticed The approximation to Round and Rondure, in the Square & triangular Forms— & that pleasure which depends on the subtle Sense of Est quod non est?—Balance: Synthesis of Antithesis?—and Secondly . . . the Polyolbiosis of each appearance from the recollection of so many others subtly combining with it / Sails bellying with Sails under reef . . . the Ideas of full Sail modifying the impression of the naked Masts, not on the eye but on the Mind, &c &c— . . . [*NC,* 2: 2061 f.26^{v}]

Coleridge nearly teases himself out of thought. Insofar as he registers an impression made "not on the eye but on the Mind," he is of course revealing the difference between words and pictures, for while the writer can say that the present and visible line of a naked mast recalls the absent curve of the full-bellying sail, the painter cannot represent an absent form without making it present. Nevertheless, the painter can represent what Coleridge has seen with his eye—"the *approximation* to Round and Rondure" in rectilinear forms.

If we ask whether this approximation can itself be "seen" and depicted or merely "felt" in the mind and evoked by language, we touch a borderline of difference between pictures and words, which are sometimes distinguished as the media of representation on the one hand and evocation on the other. Pictures give us—or seem to give us—present and visible objects, while words signify objects we are asked to remember, imagine, or conceive, and thus they convey to us the Coleridgean—or ur-Derridean—"Sense of Est quod non est." Yet all "discovery" of geometrical form in natural objects is an act of the mind as well as of the eye. In Turner's *Buttermere,* the mind of the artist makes an uncompleted circle from a rainbow and its reflection, and in turn the picture of an uncompleted circle evokes a whole one from the mind of the spectator. In *Calais Pier,* the interaction of angle and curve works like a complex series of allusions in poetry. The angle and the curve evoke the triangle and the circle, and the stability of these geometrical forms in their pure and separate state is at once threatened and energized by their intercourse with each other. The geometry of the picture, therefore, is just as much the expression of Turner's mind as it is a representation of the outside world.

IV

In Romantic poetry and painting alike, geometry is used to express a consciousness of boundaries crossed, of permanence, and of dynamic interaction. Yet its most important role, I think, is to indicate the observer's relation to the world by the angle from which he sees it. In this light, geometry serves to express at once the subjectivity and the power of the individual consciousness: of consciousness bound to the position of the eye but also bounding through it, using the personal angle of its vision to reconstruct the world.

The most vivid example of this in Romantic poetry is the boat-stealing episode in Wordsworth's *The Prelude.* I return to this episode by way of Wordsworth's theory of the sublime, which significantly emphasizes the effect of the observer's position on what he sees. Unlike Burke and Reynolds, Wordsworth did not equate sublimity with objective angularity, with the geometrical shape of the objects perceived; undulating lines, he wrote, may "convey to the mind sensations not less sublime than those which were excited by their opposites, the abrupt and the precipitous" (*PrW,* 2: 352). What mattered to Wordsworth was not the geometry of the external world but the state of the observer's mind, which was at least partly determined by the angle of his vision. Wordsworth wrote that to experience sublimity—a feeling of "exaltation or awe"—the observer must get from an object a sense of individuality, a sense of duration, and a sense of power (*PrW,* 2: 349, 351). The sense of duration is obviously something felt in the mind rather than seen, and Wordsworth links the sense of power to the "sense of motion" that the mind imputes to the stationary lines of a mountain (*PrW,* 2: 352). But the sense of individuality depends on the observer's vantage point. If, writes Wordsworth, a group of mountains

> be so distant that, while we look at them, they are only thought of as the crown of a comprehensive Landscape . . . we shall receive from them a grand impression, and nothing more. But if they be looked at from a point which has brought us so near that the mountain is almost the sole object before our eyes, yet not so near but that the whole of it is visible, we shall be impressed with a sensation of sublimity. [*PrW,* 2: 351]

The sense of individuality, therefore, depends on the angle from which a particular object is seen. And by thus determining the sense of individuality, the angle of vision helps to determine whether any object will appear sublime. In the "Essay Supplementary to the Preface [of 1815]," Wordsworth writes that poetry should "treat of things not as they *are,* but as they appear . . . as they *seem* to exist to the *senses,* and to the *passions*" (*PrW,* 3: 63). The boat-stealing episode is a study in appearance, for the angle of vision from which the boy sees the rising cliff is crucial to its impact upon him. As he rows out from beneath the craggy ridge, its summit seems at first "the bound of the horizon" (*Prelude* 1: 399), and as he looks up at this summit with a "fix'd" and steady gaze, it is clearly "the sole object before [his] eyes." He cannot see any of the cliff that stands behind it until he gets some distance from the shore. Only then does the cliff become visible at all, and when he has rowed as far from shore as he cares to, he is just approaching the point at which the whole of it would become visible, rising up between him and the stars (*Prelude* 1: 397–410). It "towered" over him—as the 1850 *Prelude* says—precisely because of the angle from which he saw it.

Turner would have understood this perfectly. If Wordsworth believed that poetry should deal with appearances, Turner believed that painting could deal with nothing else. He noted in one lecture that while geometry enables us to perceive solids, painting seeks to represent "not what are solids but what they appear to be" (TMS U f.2). And in another lecture, he declared that the laws of perspective tell the artist "how . . . to express the situation of each object, as it appears to the Eye, as well as the relative form breadth and height" (TMS M. f.1). What Turner saw was that however clear and self-possessed might be the mind behind a human eye, the eye itself—in any given moment—was subjectively bound to a particular vantage point from which the view was limited, and sometimes distorted. One of his examples is strikingly close to Wordsworth's rising cliff. In an undated addition to his third lecture, Turner observed that only when an observer's eye is approximately level with an object can he accurately and geometrically gauge its height. Suppose, he says, we were looking at St. Paul's from the lower part of Fleet Street, which offers the most distinct view possible of the front and the dome. The angle of our vision would be relatively low, yet even from this angle we could do no more than guess how far the dome rises above the front. "If thus the Eye is deceived" says Turner, "at that distance, as to its [the dome's] geometric measurements, how much the depression of the dome be expressed were we to approach it—as it would appear rapidly to decrease and at London House yard sinking below the angle of the Front" (TMS M f.23^{v}). Essentially, Turner here describes the same set of circumstances that made the cliff appear to rise up over Wordsworth. Just as the cliff appeared to rise when Wordsworth rowed away from it, so the dome of St. Paul's seems to sink as the observer approaches it, and both examples illustrate the subjectivity of perspective.

The subjectivity of perspective was for Turner an inescapable fact of vision. Echoing the Blakean axiom that "The Eye altering alters all," Turner declared: "All things are limited in a picture to the limited power of the Eye" (TMS BB 64^{v}–65). Throughout his lectures, Turner repeatedly insists that the eye naturally alters the forms of things, and that only by taking stock of this alteration can the painter hope to represent the true appearance of such forms.

Earlier theorists on perspective tried to avoid this problem by advising painters to represent objects at a distance, with the line of sight either level or pitched up at a relatively low angle. Turner would have found such advice, for instance, in Thomas Malton's *Compleat Treatise on Perspective* (1775), which was written by the father of Turner's first drawing master and which Turner used extensively in preparing his lectures. On the matter of viewpoint, Malton declares: "If the Optic Angle, under which the whole Picture is seen, exceeds 50, or at the most, 60 Degrees, the Distance is not sufficient; as the visual rays will cut the Picture very oblique, near its extremes, and occasion a disagreeable distortion of the Objects on the extreme parts of it."[18] This position seemed to Turner arbitrary and dictatorial. Though he never criticized Malton by name, he sharply attacked Malton's position. Theorists insist, he says, that "the object must not be delineated by a near point which produces distortion." But in the works of great painters, "we have to do with those very distortions, if so they must be called by Theorists."[19] And in nature itself, Turner insisted, objects are seen from every point of view:

> In Nature are they not to be look[ed] at in every angle, position, or incidence of Vision, comparatively, and are they not to be represented by the Painter because not seen under a certain angle, and are not the powers of the Painter as extensive, or more so, he that may use forms, that would be temerity in [architectural] constructions and impracticable to Sculpture, must he be confined to a certain angle of representation, or of view [?]
>
> Surely not, and those who attempt to forge such fetters to subjugate vision or enslave art rivet but another link of the chain, round the neck of such tyranny. [TMS L f.15; cf. BB f.13]

Tyranny is a strong word, but Turner had some cause to use it. By restricting the range of angles from which a scene might be depicted, parallel perspective riveted painting to the principles of plane geometry: virtually all lines in a picture were to be parallel to the horizontal or vertical lines, and the receding planes that marked the stages of depth in a picture were to be parallel to its surface.[20] Exponents of parallel perspective were dogmatic in its defense. Malton, who called it "an infallible and most exact science," roundly declared: "I will stake all my knowledge in Perspective . . . that Objects of equal magnitude, and equally distant from the Picture parallel to them, however otherwise situated or elevated will be represented equal" (*CT*, pp. 94, 96). But such a formula took no account of what happened to the appearance of objects when they were seen from certain angles. And if defenders of parallel perspective thought close-up views of tall objects would produce distortion, Turner argued that parallel perspective not only prohibited certain points of view but actually falsified the way in which things appear at any angle.

Turner's attack on parallel perspective sprang from his conviction that the field of human vision is circular. Strictly speaking, he said, nature presented "only one Horizontal and one perpendicular line" (TMS M f.22^{v}). Since all others became curved as they moved away from the center of focus, they should also curve as they move away from the center of a picture. It was therefore false, he thought, to represent even rectilinear objects as "square in all places to the Eye," or to divide a landscape or a building into "compartments Geometric" (TMS K f.15^{v}-16). The neat and symmetrical structures of geometry simply did not meet the test of vision. From certain angles, as Turner said, "Circles become Ovals Squares lozenges [and] . . . right lines appear to draw or converge together" (TMS I f.24). Parallel lines do not meet in geometry, but to the eye they appear to do so; when you approach the towers of Westminster Abbey, said Turner, so that you can just take in their height, "they rapidly decrease upwards and appear to the Eye even to incline towards each other."[21] Yet it was not only awkward angles that produced such awkward sights. "The eye," said Turner, "must take in all objects upon a Parabolic curve for in looking into space the eye cannot but receive what is within the limits of extended sight, which must form a circle to the eye."[22]

Turner's theory of curvilinear perspective graphically articulates something in which Wordsworth and Coleridge firmly believed: the creative power of the human eye. The rigid squares and "compartments Geometric" formed by parallel perspective correspond to the universe of "*little* things" that Coleridge found unintelligible, and which he longed to convert into something "*one & indivisible*" (*LC,* 1: 349). One particularly vivid example from *The Prelude* shows how curvilinear perspective can help to achieve this end. Recounting a series of boyhood experiences, Wordsworth tells us what he saw while skating along a frozen river with his friends:

> and oftentimes
> When we had given our bodies to the wind,
> And all the shadowy banks, on either side
> Came sweeping through the darkness, spinning still
> The rapid line of motion; then at once
> Have I, reclining back upon my heels,
> Stopp'd short, yet still the solitary Cliffs
> Wheeled by me, even as if the earth had roll'd
> With visible motion her diurnal round;
> Behind me did they stretch in solemn train
> Feebler and feebler, and I stood and watch'd
> Till all was tranquil as a dreamless sleep.
>
> [1: 478–89]

This is a passage of characteristically Wordsworthian daring. Abandoning the fixed "station" from which a topographical poet would typically describe a "prospect," Wordsworth gives his mind's eye to the wind, even as the boy gave his body to it. But the result is not an indistinguishable blur. It is rather a "line of motion," an arc or circle made by banks that are—or rather seem to be—"spinning still." The phrase is subtly oxymoronic; even in their apparent motion the banks are "still" because they seem to move in a constant arc. Conversely, when the boy himself is "still" or, more precisely, "stopped short," the banks continue to move. "Reclining back," the boy takes up an observer's station, but the very suddenness with which he does so leaves the world still moving around him, the cliffs "still wheeling." What the boy experienced was vertigo; what the poet creates is a vision of circularity stretching infinitely outward, from the spinning banks to the wheeling cliffs to the round and rolling earth. In the words of Turner, the whole world thus forms "a circle to the eye."

But the words of the aptly named Turner apply still more to his own later work, where—as if in reenactment of Genesis—he repeatedly turns elemental energy into circular form. A notable example is *Snowstorm: Steamboat off a Harbor's Mouth,* exhibited in 1842 (fig. 3). By Turner's own account, this was a "record" of what he witnessed from the deck of a ship caught in a snowstorm. Lashed to the mast at his own request so that he might witness the storm, he was a radically destabilized observer.[23] But

Figure 3. Turner, *Snowstorm: Steamboat off a Harbour's Mouth*. (The Tate Gallery, London. Reprinted by permission.)

even as Wordsworth turns the eye of a dizzy skater into the still point of a wheeling earth, Turner projects his own eye into the paddle wheel of the steamboat. Fixed in the very center of the whirling elements, the paddle wheel is an antisun, the dark and steady pupil around which all else revolves.

Unlike Wordsworth's skating scene, however, Turner's *Snowstorm* is not simply organized as a series of concentric circles. Most of its major lines are nearly straight: the steamboat's mast, the diagonal underside of the smoke above it, the slanting horizon that cuts across the middle of the picture, and the intersecting diagonals in the waves at lower left. These lines suggest a vortex because we are made to see them as lines of centrifugal force driving outward from a center of whirling energy. Conspicuous by their absence are the two lines indispensable to parallel perspective: the horizontal and the vertical. Where we look for the vertical, we find a bowed and slanted mast; where we look for a level horizon, we find another slant with a curve at the end: a more emphatic version of the sloping horizontal that Coleridge noted in 1803. The slanting horizon is undoubtedly a "record" of what Turner saw from the tossing vessel, yet more than anything else in the picture, perhaps, it is also his crowning act of defiance toward the doctrines of parallel perspective. Thirteen years earlier, he had exhibited a painting called *Ulysses Deriding Polyphemus.* This time, lashed to a mast at his own request, he became his own Ulysses, and what he produced might well be called *Turner Deriding Malton.* Against rectilinear rigidity he sets the curvilinear form of human vision, and against the objective transcript of the way things are he sets the subjective re-creation of the way they seem.

Turner believed that he could render the power of natural forces only by subjecting himself and his vision to them, only by making a snowstorm—in Wordsworth's terms—"the sole object before his eyes." Yet the act of subjection was also an act of conquest. By the subjective power of his own vision, he made a rounded whole of raging elements, so that for all their turbulence, they nonetheless suggest the transcendent perfection of the circle. The circle in turn asserts its power not by consuming straight lines but by setting them in motion, animating what would otherwise be static parallels and perpendiculars. The abandonment of parallel for curvilinear perspective, therefore, is an abandonment of rigidity for dynamism, and of finitude for infinitude. So long as we can look down on a scene, so long as we can gauge its measurements confidently by the laws of parallel perspective, it remains for us fixed and finite. But when a mountain looms up over us, as the huge cliff loomed up over Wordsworth, it is fixed and finite no more. "Parallel lines," wrote Turner, "carry with them no idea of hight while the Oblique one may rise to infinity." In the latter case, altitude is not a product of calculation but "the natural feeling of the mind" (TMS K f.14).

The feeling of the mind—the mind's consciousness of infinity—is precisely what the English Romantic geometry of the infinite is meant to convey. Essentially, it is a geometry created by a mind working through the eye. Wordsworth wrote, about 1798:

> There is creation in the eye
> Nor less in all the other senses; powers

> They are that colour, model, and combine
> The things perceived with such an absolute
> Essential energy that we may say
> That those most godlike faculties of ours
> At one and the same moment are the mind
> And the mind's minister.[24]

When he thus declares the power of the human eye, Wordsworth speaks for Coleridge, Turner, and Constable, too, I think, as well as for himself. It was they who created the geometry of the infinite, who saw both limit and limitlessness, who caught from evanescent phenomena the permanence of implied geometrical figures, who found in matter's mouldering structures the pure forms of circle, triangle, cube, and square. It was they who perceived the vital interaction of angle and curve, and who, to represent that interaction in poetry and painting, replaced the line of undulating beauty by a line of complex power. And it was they, finally, who gauged the influence of the eye on natural objects. Instead of receiving the world as a rectilinear grid, the energy of the eye re-creates it as a rounded whole. Giving up the superior vantage point from which it may literally look down upon a scene of finite, ordered parallels, the eye submits itself to the immeasurable sublimity of towering cliffs and raging storms. But in the very act of giving up its sovereignty over a geometrically determinate universe, the eye discovers a godlike power to elevate natural forms, to delineate the very structure of their motions, and to perpetuate their evanescent character. Radically redefined as it was by the vital energies of landscape and powers of the human eye, geometry became the measure by which the English Romantic poets and painters re-created the measureless power of landscape.

Notes

1. Alastair Fowler, "Periodization and Interart Analogies," *New Literary History* 3, no. 3 (Spring 1972); 506—cited hereafter as "Periodization."

2. Meyer Schapiro, "Style," in *Anthropology Today,* ed. Alfred Kroeber (Chicago: University of Chicago Press, 1952), p. 288.

3. *Complete Works of William Hazlitt,* ed. P. P. Howe (London: J. M. Dent & Sons, 1930–34), 16: 63—cited hereafter as *CWH.*

4. *CWH,* 16: 64. In speaking of Augustan critics, I refer particularly to Joshua Reynolds and Edmund Burke. In the *Discourses,* Reynolds repeatedly urges painters to be "poetical" in their subject matter but not in their style, for to imitate the sugges-

tiveness of poetry, he says, would be to violate an "indispensable" rule of painting: "that everything shall be carefully and distinctly expressed." *Discourses on Art,* ed. Robert Wark (San Marino, Calif.: Huntington Library, 1959), p. 164—hereafter cited as *D.* Burke takes a similar line in his analysis of the sublime and the beautiful, where he describes painting as a medium of clear and beautiful representation, and poetry—or simply language—as a medium of obscure and sublime suggestion. See *A Philosophical Enquiry into the Origin of Our Ideas of the Sublime and the Beautiful,* ed. J. T. Boulton (Notre Dame, Ind.: University of Notre Dame Press, 1958), pp. 60, 174—cited hereafter as *SB.*

5. Quoted in "Periodization," pp. 498–99. For a recent discussion of the significance of indeterminacy in Romantic poetry, especially in Wordsworth, see Thomas Weiskel, *The Romantic Sublime: Studies in the Structure and Psychology of Transcendence* (Baltimore, Md.: Johns Hopkins University Press, 1976), pp. 26–30, 167–204.

6. *Biographia Literaria,* ed. J. T. Shawcross (London: Oxford University Press, 1907), 1: 59—hereafter cited as *BL;* and *CWH,* 4: 76n.

7. See for instance Lawrence Gowing, *Turner: Imagination and Reality* (New York: The Museum of Modern Art, 1966), p. 31—hereafter cited as *TIR.*

8. A. M. Holcomb, "'Indistinctness is my fault': A Letter about Turner from C. R. Leslie to James Lenox," *Burlington Magazine* 114 (1972): 557–58.

9. *The Prose Works of William Wordsworth,* ed. W. J. B. Owen and Jane Worthington Smyser (Oxford: Clarendon Press, 1974), 2: 354—hereafter cited as *PrW;* and *The Letters of William and Dorothy Wordsworth: The Later Years,* ed. Ernest De Selincourt (Oxford: Clarendon Press, 1939), 1: 134–35.

10. *The Prelude: or, Growth of a Poet's Mind,* ed. Ernest De Selincourt, 2d ed., rev. by Helen Darbishire (Oxford: Clarendon Press, 1959)—hereafter cited as *The Prelude.* Unless otherwise noted, I quote from the text of 1805–06.

11. *The Notebooks of Samuel Taylor Coleridge,* ed. Kathleen Coburn (Princeton, N.J.: Princeton University Press, 1957—), 2: 2346—hereafter cited as *NC.*

12. British Museum Additional Manuscripts 46151, M f.22—hereafter cited as TMS. In his first lecture, Turner says that without "the geometrical laws of perspective," art "totters at its very foundation" (TMS K1^{v}–K6^{v}).

13. TMS K f.23. Taking some freedom with the punctuation, Turner quotes from the revised version of *The Pleasures of the Imagination,* Book 2 (1765), ll. 133–38.

14. William Hogarth, *The Analysis of Beauty,* ed. J. Burke (Oxford: The Clarendon Press, 1955), pp. 54–55, 76, 158–59, 183.

15. See, for instance, *NC* 1: 227, 335 f.3^{v}, 418 f.29, 1220 f.19^{v}, 1496 f.69, 1477 f.39, and 1800 f.92^{v}.

16. *NC,* 1: 1211 f.7^{v}; 2: 2343. In *Fragment of an Essay on Beauty* (1818), Coleridge writes: "As to lines, the rectilineal are in themselves the lifeless, the determined *ab extra,* but still in immediate union with the cycloidal, which are expressive of function. The curve line is a modification of the force from without by the force from within, or the spontaneous" (*BL,* 2: 251).

17. *NC* 1: 1489 f.59^{v}, 1449 f.6^{v}, and 1482 f.40^{v}. See also *NC* 1: 1457 f.12^{v}, 1489 f.52^{v}, and 2: 2690 f.89^{v}–90.

18. *A Compleat Treatise on Perspective in Theory and Practice: On the True Principles of Dr. Brook Taylor* (London, 1778), pp. 96–97—hereafter cited as *CT.* Reynolds makes a similar point in his tenth Discourse; see *D,* p. 186.

19. TMS L f.14^{v}–15.

20. I am drawing here on John Joshua Kirby, *Dr. Brook Taylor's Method of Perspective Made Easy Both in Theory and Practice* (London, 1754), pp. 23–24; *CT,* p. 47; and J. W.

Alston, *Hints to Young Practitioners in the Study of Landscape,* 3d ed. (London, [1804]), pp. 11–15.

21. TMS M f.25–25^{v}. Coleridge likewise noted that a precipice loses its perpendicularity when seen from close range: see *NC,* 1: 825 f.62.

22. Quoted in Jack Lindsay, *J. M. W. Turner: His Life and Work* (Greenwich, Conn.: New York Graphic Society, 1966), p. 115.

23. For the factual circumstances mentioned here, see *TIR,* pp. 45–48.

24. *Poetical Works,* ed. Ernest De Selincourt and Helen Darbishire (Oxford: Clarendon Press, 1949), 5: 343.

Alexander Pope and *Picturesque* Landscape

James R. Aubrey

United States Air Force Academy

THE word *picturesque* today often suggests quaint poverty—an old man sitting on the steps of a shanty, or a broken windmill on an abandoned farm. When the word entered the language, however, picturesque referred to scenery that was like a picture, especially a picture by one of the seventeenth-century painters whose charmingly various landscapes helped to wean British taste away from the mazes, geometrical walks, and sculpted shrubbery of Continental formal gardens. One of the first to promote the idea of looking at natural landscape for pleasure, for what we would call an aesthetic response, was Joseph Addison. He used the terms *beautiful, great,* and *uncommon* to describe three kinds of scenery that provide "pleasures of the imagination" to an onlooker.[1] The term *beautiful* did not change in the eighteenth century, but *sublime* replaced *great,* and what Addison called "uncommon" scenes eventually became known as "picturesque." The informal arrangements and natural shapes of picturesque landscape became the fashionable norm in gardening by midcentury, and the so-called English country garden still shapes our expectations when we walk through parks.

Alexander Pope helped to popularize the idea of landscape gardening, and visitors assure us that his estate at Twickenham had thick foliage and the requisite broken views, but his garden is usually described as "transitional," "emblematic," or "poetic," rather than picturesque. John Searle's diagram (fig. 1) certainly brings out the regularity more than the variety. The irregular

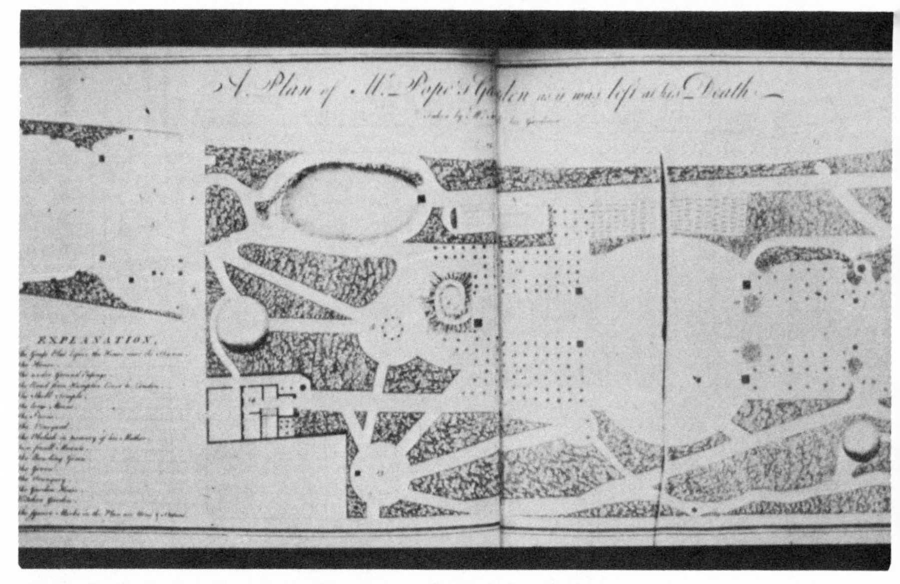

Figure 1. John Searle's diagram of Twickenham.

paths around the perimeter seem only a tentative step away from formal garden symmetry, and we might imagine that Christopher Hussey was right in 1925 when he wrote that Pope had "little appreciation for the Picturesque."[2] Norman Ault raised doubts about Hussey's assessment in 1949 when he pointed out that Pope "was the first to use the word [picturesque] with any frequency in English."[3] Morris Brownell went further in his book *Alexander Pope and the Arts of Georgian England,* which shows not only that Pope was extremely sensible to picturesque landscape but also that he, instead of William Kent, deserves to be recognized as the inventor of the landscape garden concept.[4] I agree that Pope was a setter more than a follower of fashionable tastes, but we should not overlook one important qualification: even when he seems to be responding to perceptual pleasures, Pope subordinates his esteem for picturesque landscape to moral considerations.

The word *picturesque* had two meanings in the early eighteenth century, and Pope was aware of both. The more traditional meaning of picturesque was "vividly graphic," possessing what the Greeks called *enargeia.*[5] Pope used picturesque in this sense in one of his notes to *The Iliad.* When the Trojans are setting fire to some of the Greek ships, Patroclus prostrates himself before the ship of Achilles, pours out his tears, and tells Achilles that he is "harder than the Rocks of the Sea which lie in Prospect before them, if he is not touch'd with so moving a spectacle." Pope comments: "As nothing can be more natural and affecting than the Speech of *Patroclus,* so nothing is more lively and Picturesque than the Attitude he is here describ'd in."[6] Pope clearly does not refer to the landscape but to the pose of the human figure in the foreground as "picturesque," because the moment is climactic and worthy of being "pictured" by a painter of Homer's narrative. Pope once recommended that his friend Ralph Allen buy a comparable narrative painting, Nicolas Poussin's *The Death of Germanicus* (fig. 2), as "prophane History," to balance the sacred history paintings Allen already had in his house.[7] Pope was more emphatic in a letter to the portraitist Charles Jervas: "I long to see you a History Painter. You have already done enough for the Private,

Figure 2. Nicolas Poussin, *The Death of Germanicus.*

Figure 3. Claude Lorrain, *Seaport*.

do something for the Publick." Pope seems to have considered heroic narratives to be the highest kind of painting, the visual equivalent of epic poems.[8]

The other meaning of picturesque, one that was becoming increasingly fashionable during Pope's life, had to do with landscape that pleases the eye with its variety of light and shade. Picturesque in this sense, too, means "like a picture"—not a narrative or history painting but a landscape painting in the manner of Salvator Rosa, Gaspar Dughet, or Claude Lorrain.[9] A passage from Pope's 1711 *Temple of Fame* seems to allude to paintings such as Claude's *Seaport* (fig. 3):

> Here sailing Ships delight the wand'ring Eyes;
> There Trees, and intermingl'd Temples rise:
> Now a clear Sun the shining Scene displays,
> The transient Landscape now in Clouds decays.[10]

Although "seascape" might be a more precise label than "landscape," the idea of a "shining Scene" is central to all paintings by Claude, who art historians say "was the first artist to paint the sun—but a sun whose dazzling rays do not abolish space."[11] Claude does not rely so much on the converging linear perspective of his buildings to convey depth as he does on a hazy atmosphere that affects the colors. Pope once referred to this technique, called aerial perspective, when he told Joseph Spence that in gardening "you may distance things by darkening them."[12] By mixing black with the colors on the palette a painter can tone down the hues as the atmosphere does over a distance, to give the buildings in the background of *Seaport* a gray pallor, for example. In the same way, darker trees at the end of a carefully planned garden prospect can convey a sense of landscape through the illusion of greater depth.

Pope's use of the word picturesque in a 1712 letter is cited by the *OED* as one of the word's earliest appearances in English. Pope observes:

> Mr. Philips has two lines which seem to me what the French call very *picturesque,* that I cannot omit to you—
>
> All hid in snow, in bright confusion lie,
> And with one dazling waste fatigue the eye.[13]

Around 1728, according to Spence, Pope illustrated "that idea of 'picturesque'" with the example of a "swan just gilded with the sun amidst the shade of a tree over the water on the Thames."[14] The second image is much more Claude-like than the first, but in both cases what Pope is calling picturesque are scenes that strike the eye to produce perceptual pleasure—not scenes with the kind of moral beauty conveyed by Patroclus, pictured in his noble attitude.

Like Pope, who used picturesque in both senses, Claude produced both moralized narrative paintings and landscape paintings for the sake of the prospect alone. *Pastoral Landscape* (fig. 4) is a representative example of the paintings that helped set the standard for picturesque gardening. The composition generally includes dark trees framing the foreground, which contains figures who help to set the intended mood—elegiac, festive, or perhaps in this case one of Virgilian contentment. The middle distance is lighter and typically contains water and an arched bridge. Some architectural feature usually terminates the view. As in *Seaport,* the prospect is lit from behind making the horizon hazy and softening the outlines of objects.

Figure 4. Claude Lorrain, *Pastoral Landscape*.

Pope's 1731 poem about architecture and gardening, *Epistle IV: To Burlington,* is best known for its satiric sketch of Timon's Villa, where "each alley has a brother" and one finds "trees cut to statues, statues thick as trees." Other parts of the poem, however, are a virtual manifesto for the picturesque revolution in gardening, like this piece of advice to the landscapist:

> He gains all points, who pleasingly confounds,
> Surprizes, varies, and conceals the Bounds.
>   Consult the Genius of the Place in all;
> That tells the Waters or to rise, or fall,
> Or helps th' ambitious Hill the Heav'n to scale,
> Or scoops in circling theatres the Vale,
> Calls in the Country, catches opening glades,
> Joins willing woods, and varies shades from shades,
> Now breaks or now directs, th' intending Lines;
> Paints as you plant, and, as you work, designs.[15]

When Pope praises gardens that "pleasingly confound," he is endorsing what Addison calls "pleasures of the imagination" that accompany the sight of an "uncommon," or "picturesque," landscape. The gardens that please most are those that "call in the country" by "concealing the bounds" so that the landscape outside the cultivated garden becomes a part of the view, like the background of a landscape painting. In the last couplet I quoted, Pope invites us to see that very analogy, between painting and gardening, when he turns the genius of the landscape into an inventive artist who "paints as you plant," and the gardener into something of a studio assistant.

The analogy between gardening and painting was fundamental to the picturesque movement. Pope expressed the relation baldly in 1734, when he told Spence "all gardening is landscape painting."[16] According to at least one critic, James Thomson was the first to recognize a triple sisterhood of the arts of painting, poetry, and gardening in 1735.[17] Even if the idea was not a commonplace before the 1730s, the relation seems to have occurred long before to Pope, who as early as 1706 compared a piece of beautiful countryside to a beautiful poem or painting, each capable of being defaced by the hand of man:

> In Poetry as in Painting, a Man may lay Colours one upon another, till they stiffen and deaden the Piece. But to bestow heightning on every part is monstrous: Some parts ought to be lower than the rest; and nothing looks more ridiculous, than a Work, where the Thoughts, however different in their own nature, seem all on a level: 'Tis like a Meadow newly mown, where *Weeds, Grass,* and *Flowers* are laid even, and appear undistinguish'd.[18]

True, mowing is not gardening, but Pope here is imparting to a varied landscape the kind of beauty found in the traditional sister arts of poetry and painting, and he discusses the results of mowing as if the leveling could help to explain the clouded judgment of a bad artist who gilds everything. Pope is taking for granted analogies among landscape, poetry, and painting long before the supposed "discovery" of the relation and also is implying an appreciation for meadows several years before sensibility to picturesque landscape was to become fashionable.

Also worth noting is Pope's implied praise of the meadow's beauty before it is mown in terms of levels, of "heightning" and lowering. These criteria for judging beauty aren't wholly compatible with notions of the picturesque. If we compare two avant-garde statements, by Pope and by Addison, we can see

Pope's old-fashioned ideas still there. In 1712 Addison wrote in *The Spectator:*

> Delightful Scenes, whether in Nature, Painting, or Poetry, have a kindly Influence on the Body, as well as the Mind, and not only serve to clear and brighten the Imagination, but are able to disperse Grief and Melancholly, and to set the Animal Spirits in pleasing and agreeable Motions.[19]

According to Addison, delightful scenes are those that please the imagination, and he elaborates on the psychology of those effects. In 1713, one year later, Pope wrote an influential essay for the *Guardian* in which he mocked the use of topiary in gardens and, like Addison, praised natural landscape:

> There is certainly something in the amiable Simplicity of unadorned Nature, that spreads over the Mind a more noble Sort of Tranquility, and a loftier Sensation of Pleasure, than can be raised from the nicer Scenes of Art.[20]

Pope's praise of "unadorned nature" aligns him with Addison against formal gardens, but not for quite the same reasons. Addison praises any scene that produces pleasures of the imagination, but Pope adds morally charged qualifiers when he endorses only the "loftier" sensations or the "more noble" sorts of tranquillity. Both men like picturesque gardens, but Pope considers them to be inherently of a higher quality than formal gardens, whose excess of artistry, as Pope remarks in his preface to *The Iliad,* "can only reduce the beauties of Nature to more regularity, and such a Figure, which the common Eye may better take in, and is therefore more entertain'd with."[21] For Pope, a landscape garden—like a meadow before it is mown—is apparently something like a Georgic, and the formal garden like a lesser kind of poetry—an acrostic, perhaps. Unlike Addison, who locates the standard of pleasure inside the mind, Pope evaluates gardens in terms of the external standards of Renaissance criticism, the kinds and hierarchies of high and low art.

Pope's understanding of picturesque landscape in terms of traditional ideas about art gave him a basis for judging a landscape garden not only in terms of the pleasures of imagination it produces but also in terms of the moral values it expresses. In his letter recommending *The Death of Germanicus,* Pope goes on to observe about history paintings: "A Man not only shews his Taste but his Virtue, in the Choice of such Ornaments."[22] Likewise, a garden reveals the character of its owner, and judgments of beauty, especially for Pope, are combined with judgments of morals—taste and virtue—as if the landscape garden were the setting of a history painting about the owner who, like Patroclus, occupies the foreground and is the true subject.

Pope's attitude reveals itself in a 1724 letter describing Robert Digby's estate, Sherborne. The terrain there is naturally irregular, and Pope writes to Martha Blount that Sherborne is "so peculiar and its situation of so uncommon a kind, that it merits a more particular description." Pope takes Mrs. Blount on an epistolary walk through the house and the park, within sight of crumbling bridges and sound of a cascading stream, to the ruined castle that Pope says "compleats the Solemnity of the Scene" (fig. 5). As he describes the ruins, Pope digresses about ways that Digby could make their appearance more picturesque by planting "Greens and Parterres from part to part," trees in some of the open rooms to make "a natural Tapistry to the walls," and turf around the outside to provide "a bold Basement to show it." Pope also mentions that paths of earth or sand built under vantage points in the wall could aid a climber to obtain framed picturelike views. As he imagines these improvements, Pope is led to envision an essentially Claudian prospect nearby, remarkably similar to Claude's *Pastoral Landscape.* Referring to potential improvements at Sherborne, Pope continues:

> I could very much wish this were done as well as a little Temple built on a neighboring round Hill that is seen from all points of the Garden & is extremely pretty. It would finish some Walks, & particularly be a fine Termination to the River to be seen from the Entrance into the Deep Scene I have describd by the Cascade where it would appear as in the clouds, between the tops of some very lofty Trees that form an Arch before it, with a great Slope downward to the end of the said river.[23]

This imaginary scene is the climax of Pope's description of the estate. For Morris Brownell, Pope's enthusiasm for Sherborne and his interest in broken views reveal acute sensibility and an avant-garde eye for the picturesque. In a detailed study of the estate, Peter Martin points out that "the combination of formal-

Figure 5. Robert Digby's estate, Sherborne.

ity, variety, irregularity, wilderness of Sherborne was in 1724 unique, and that Pope indeed recognized the fact."[24] What neither writer acknowledges is that the picturesque improvement Pope recommends just before his flight of Claudian fancy, he takes back immediately afterwards. His letter goes on to praise Digby for *not* "beautifying" the ruins with paths and plantings, picturesque as those changes might be:

> What should induce My Lord D. the rather to cultivate these ruins and do honour to them, is that they do no small honour to his Family; that Castle, which was very ancient, being demolished in the Civil wars after it was nobly defended by one of his Ancestors in the cause of the King. I would sett up at the Entrance of 'em an Obelisk, with an inscription of the Fact: which would be a Monument erected to the very Ruins; as the adorning & beautifying them in the manner I have been imagining, would not be unlike the Egyptian Finery of bestowing Ornament and curiosity on dead bodies.

Pope goes on to praise Digby's character, concluding that "his Tenants live almost as happy & contented as himself." Pope's reflections on Sherborne bring to his mind Digby's ancestors, one of whom was Sir Walter Raleigh, and in turn the noble qualities of Digby himself. To be sure, Pope values a picturesque landscape, but he values even more highly the moral qualities of its owner and wants them in the "picture."

Pope's urge to assign a higher importance to such moral values, external to the picturesque scene at Sherborne, leads me to question whether the usual assumption, that Claude's landscape paintings provide the closest visual analogy to picturesque landscape gardens, indeed describes Pope's ideal. To him, landscape painting for the sake of landscape alone probably seemed insufficiently moralized to be great art, as Sherborne would have seemed without the moralizing presence of Digby and his family's achievement in the "foreground." The distinction Pope seems to draw, even if it is not fully conscious, resembles a distinction more carefully drawn by Roger de Piles in his 1708 *Cours de peinture.* "Among the many different styles of landskip," de Piles wrote, "I shall confine myself to two; *the heroick,* and *the pastoral* or *rural;* for all other styles are but mixtures of these." De Piles goes on to describe Claude Lorrain as a pastoral painter of "nature simple, without ornament, and without artifice; but with all those graces with which she adorns herself much more, when left to herself, than when constrained by art." De Piles describes Nicolas Poussin, on the other hand, as a successful painter in the "heroick style," which draws "both from art and nature, everything that is great and extraordinary in either" in order to present nature "as we think she ought to be."[25] I believe that Poussin's landscapes, rather than Claude's, more accurately correspond to Pope's vision of what a landscape garden ought to be.

De Piles undoubtedly had in mind two of Poussin's most famous paintings, the Phocion landscapes. In *The Body of Phocion Carried out of Athens* (fig. 6), for example, we see a landscape painting whose narrative subject makes it also a history painting. According to Plutarch, Phocion was a model of civic virtue. In his youth he had been trained by Plato, and he applied the principles of his philosophy to every action, private or public, even when he knew that his view would be met with general disapproval. Phocion was finally accused of treason by his enemies in the lower classes of Athens, however, and was sentenced to death by hemlock.[26] As a further disgrace, his burial

Figure 6. Nicolas Poussin, *The Body of Phocion Carried out of Athens.*

within Athens was forbidden, and Poussin here depicts the bearing of the corpse through the countryside. A contrast to the idea of intemperate city government, the landscape conveys a sense of order by means of interlocking, geometrical patches of terrain that, like the buildings, guide one's reflections to thoughts of political harmony. Even details such as the procession to the temple of Zeus contribute to a theme of hierarchical order and justify the label "heroic landscape."[27]

The Phocion landscapes seem a closer visual analogy to Pope's line in *To Burlington,* "parts answ'ring parts shall slide into a whole" (l. 66), than do Claude's indirect evocations of tranquil moods through hazy scenes. Baudet engraved the Phocion landscapes in 1684, but we cannot be sure that Pope ever saw those particular works. Perhaps direct influence need not be an issue, however. In a discussion of Pope's *Pastorals,* Pat Rogers observes that "it could be said with total prudence that the habits of mind exemplified in Poussin were still available to the poet."[28] I claim no more—only that Pope and Poussin were spiritual brothers who shared many assumptions about the aims of art. Pope practiced all three sister arts; given his regard for epic poetry and history painting, we should not be surprised to learn that he prefers heroic to picturesque landscape.

In gardening matters, then, where Pope considered himself to be an avant-garde man of taste—where we, too, may be tempted to see him as less conservative, or even as a proto-Romantic shaper of fashions—Pope reveals his instincts to have been those of a late-Renaissance man. In *Epistle IV: To Burlington,* Pope praises the man "who plants like Bathurst, or who builds like Boyle," two of his close friends (l. 178). Just as Bathurst and his estate containing 5,000 acres of oak forests could be described as a heroic norm for landscape values in that poem, Pope's satirical sketch of Timon's pretentious villa with its formal garden might be described as mock-heroic landscape painting, in verse, with Timon as the ridiculous mock-hero in the foreground of his estate. His

> building is a Town,
> His pond an Ocean, his parterre a Down:
> Who but must laugh, the Master when he sees,
> A puny insect, shiv'ring at a breeze!
>
> [ll. 105–8]

In *The Garden and the City,* Maynard Mack describes Pope at Twickenham as "A Poet in his Landscape."[29] Pope is also "a hero in his landscape," for he viewed his garden as the setting for a Poussin-like "heroic landscape" and himself, like Phocion, the moral exemplum, or hero, in the foreground.

Notes

1. Joseph Addison and Richard Steele, *The Spectator,* ed. Donald F. Bond, 5 vols. (Oxford: Clarendon Press, 1965), 3: 540 (no. 412).

2. Christopher Hussey, *The Picturesque* (New York: Putnam, 1927), p. 30.

3. Norman Ault, *New Light on Pope* (London: Methuen, 1949), p. 80.

4. Morris Brownell, *Alexander Pope and the Arts of Georgian England* (Oxford: Clarendon Press, 1978), pp. 100, 182.

5. Walter John Hipple, Jr., *The Beautiful, the Sublime, and the Picturesque in Eighteenth-Century British Aesthetic Theory* (Carbondale: Southern Illinois University Press, 1957), p. 186; Jean Hagstrum, *The Sister Arts* (Chicago: University of Chicago Press, 1958), p. 11.

6. *The Twickenham Edition of the Poems of Alexander Pope,* ed. John Butt et al. (New

Haven: Yale University Press, 1950–69), 8: 234 (headnote to Book 16). Hereafter *Poems*.

7. *The Correspondence of Alexander Pope,* ed. George Sherburn, 5 vols. (Oxford: Clarendon Press, 1956) 4: 20. Hereafter *Corr.*

8. *Corr.* 1: 377.

9. Elizabeth Wheeler Manwaring, *Italian Landscape in Eighteenth-Century England* (New York: Oxford University Press, 1925), passim.

10. *Poems* 2:246, ll. 17–20.

11. Jacques Thuillier and Albert Chatelet, *French Painting,* trans. James Emmons (Geneva: Skira, 1964), p. 53.

12. Joseph Spence, *Observations, Anecdotes, and Characters of Books and Men,* ed. James M. Osborne, 2 vols. (Oxford: Clarendon Press, 1966), 1: 253 (no. 610). Hereafter Spence.

13. *Corr.* 1: 167–68.

14. Spence, no. 613, p. 254.

15. *Poems* 3 (pt. 2): 138–39, ll. 55–64. Subsequent references to this poem by line number.

16. Spence, no. 606, p. 252.

17. Peter Willis, "Lord Burlington and Landscape Design," *Apollo of the Arts* (Nottingham: Nottingham University Art Gallery, 1973), p. 13.

18. *Corr.* 1: 18–19.

19. Addison and Steele, *Spectator,* 3: 539 (no. 411).

20. *The Prose Works of Alexander Pope,* ed. Norman Ault (1936; reprint. ed., New York: Barnes & Noble, 1968), p. 145.

21. *Poems* 7:3.

22. *Corr.* 4:13.

23. *Corr.* 2: 239.

24. Brownell, *Alexander Pope,* p. 117; Martin, "Intimations of the New Gardening," *Garden History* 4, no. 1 (1976): 59.

25. Roger de Piles, "The Principles of Painting," trans. "A Painter, London 1743," in *A Documentary History of Art,* ed. Elizabeth Gilmore Holt (New York: Doubleday, 1958), 2: 178.

26. Anthony Blunt, "The Heroic and the Ideal Landscape in the Works of Nicolas Poussin," *Journal of the Warburg and Courtauld Institute* 7 (1944): 158.

27. Walter Friedlaender, *Nicolas Poussin* (New York: Abrams, n.d.), p. 176.

28. Pat Rogers, "Rhythm and Recoil in Pope's *Pastorals,*" *Eighteenth-Century Studies* 14 (Fall 1980): 6.

29. Maynard Mack, *The Garden and the City* (Toronto: University of Toronto Press, 1969), chap. 1.

The Arts and Society

The Metamorphosis of the Centaur in Fifth-Century Greek Arts and Society

Krin Gabbard

State University of New York, Stony Brook

STORIES about Centaurs are as old as any tale in Greek literature: Homer mentions the Centaur Chiron, Achilles' wise and virtuous tutor, as the possessor of medical knowledge (*Iliad* 11.831 and 4.219) and as the original donor of the great ash spear Peleus passed on to his son (*Iliad* 16.143 = 19.390); in the *Odyssey* Antinous the suitor warns the disguised Odysseus not to follow the example of the Centaur Eurytion, who abused hospitality when he and the other beasts attacked the Lapiths at the wedding feast of Pirithous (*Odyssey* 21.295ff.); and Archilochus knew of the Centaur Nessus, who attacked Deianira and was killed by Heracles (Dio Chrysostom 60, *init.*). In art the same stories appear on vases dating to the seventh century B.C.[1] These basic myths—involving both good and bad Centaurs—remain largely unchanged until the fourth century B.C. when Centaurs become for the first time indiscriminately combined with Satyrs and Maenads in the train of Dionysus's revelers.

Scholars offer many explanations for the existence of Centaurs in literature and art, but I have found the most useful to be that of G. S. Kirk, who has called the Centaur "a peculiarly Greek phenomenon—and there are few other parts of Greek mythology of which that can be said."[2] Kirk is quite interested in Cyclopes as well as Centaurs: both can be gentle or violent depending on which of several legends one reads. Drawing heavily upon Lévi-Strauss's theory that myth is mediation between opposites, Kirk finds Centaurs and Cyclopes to be excellent examples of how the *nomos/physis* contrast informs much of myth-making. *Nomos* is Greek for man's law or custom, *physis* for nature or natural law. Kirk points to "the extreme of culture" represented by Chiron and "nature in its most unpredictable and anti-cultural form" in the rest of the Centaurs as the embodiment of this *nomos/physis* dichotomy—a good comparison since nature can be friendly or hostile to man depending on the circumstances.[3]

Kirk offers compelling explanations for the Centaur's signification and his fascination for the Greek mind. However, my intention is not only to reveal specific associations that the Centaur held for Greeks in the years just after the retreat of the Persians in 479 B.C., but also to show how these associations changed during the following forty years. In order to explore the changing meaning of the Centaur, I will make synchronic comparisons between important works of writers and sculptors who depicted Centaurs in both the Early Classical and Mature Classical periods.

Just after the defeat of the Persians, the centauromachy at the feast for the Lapith king Pirithous and his bride Deidamia became an extremely popular subject in Greek art. In addition to a sudden upsurge in the number of vases decorated with impressions of this story, a large mural in the Theseum in Athens depicted the conflict in a version painted by Polygnotus or Micon.[4] The mural and the Theseum itself are now lost, but the painting probably provided the model for the great west pediment, still largely preserved, of the Temple of Zeus at Olympia.

The Olympia sculptures were executed between 468 and 456 and show grotesque Centaurs attacking Greek men and women who wear the dignified, restrained expressions that were characteristic of the Early Classical period. In the center of the pediment, standing tall and righteous, Apollo urges on the Greek warriors Pirithous and Theseus, who flank him on both sides. The Lapith women who are being attacked by Centaurs have calm faces that sharply contrast with the bushy beards, pointed ears, and abundant facial creases of the Centaurs.[5]

In much the same spirit, Pindar speaks of Centaurs in *Pythian 2,* dated variously from 477 to 468,[6] calling them "an offspring unhonored either among men or amid the ordinances of the gods" (*Pythian* 2.43). Pindar's fragment 166 (Sandys) also alludes to the battle at the Lapith wedding feast: "But when the beasts sensed the over-powering odor of the honeyed wine, with their hands they thrust the white milk from the tables. Uninvited, they drank out of the silver horns and began to wander in mind."

Both Pindar and the Olympia sculptors depict the Centaurs as hubristic marauders, hated by the gods, in conflict with the forces of civilization as symbolized by the Lapiths. The Greeks of the early fifth century regarded Persians in much the same way. Aeschylus makes it clear that the Persians, and especially their leader Xerxes, were unable to defeat the outnumbered Greek armies because hubris had led the invaders into *ate* and a number of disastrous acts (*Persians* 821ff.). The sudden popularity of Centaurs in art works after 479 can largely be explained by the lessons that were learned from the wars as well as by the usual chauvinism from which even the Greeks were not exempt. The centauromachy, like the gigantomachy and the amazonomachy, stood for the victory of the forces of civilization, reason and *sophrosyne* over the forces of lawlessness, disorder, and lack of self-restraint. The Lapiths were early Greeks, and their victory over the Centaurs symbolized the ascent of Greek civilization over both the ravages of nature and the intrusions of "barbaric" peoples.

Many of the changes that took place in Athens between the Persian and Peloponnesian Wars are reflected in the art and literature of the 440s: the Centaurs in Mature Classical sculpture and tragedy are not like those we have just considered. Let us examine, in some detail now, the Centaurs in Sophocles' *Trachiniae* and in the series of south metopes along the outer wall of the Athenian Parthenon. Both the play and the metopes can be dated to the decade between 448 and 438.[7]

A Centaur figures prominently in the plot of Sophocles' *Trachiniae*. As we know from legend, the Centaur Nessus offered to ferry Deianira across the river Evenus. When he laid a lustful hand upon her, her newly acquired husband, Heracles, promptly killed him. In early, painted representations of this story, Heracles kills Nessus with his sword or club. It is likely that Sophocles altered this myth, having Heracles send an arrow tipped with venom from the Hydra into the lungs of Nessus, thereby allowing time for the Centaur to instruct Deianira to collect some blood from his wound before Heracles could arrive and finish him with his sword. She was then to apply the blood to a coat that, when worn by Heracles, would ensure her husband's fidelity to her. It is also likely that Sophocles substantially altered the character of Deianira, whose name means "destroyer of men." In earlier versions of the story she gives the poisoned *chiton* to Heracles, probably with full knowledge of its powers, when Heracles returns with Iole as his concubine. Sophocles was the first writer to unite the separate incidents by means of Nessus's blood. This means that in the *Trachiniae* Deianira is blameless, and Nessus becomes the crucial link in the chain of events that cause Heracles' death.[8]

Sophocles' Nessus does not fit neatly into either of the two categories that ancient myth established for Centaurs. The traditional hubristic beasts do not seem to have the power of speech and answer only to their most immediate desires. The Nessus of earlier tradition might be of this type, but not the Nessus created by Sophocles. The subtle and clever plan that Nessus tells Deianira in the *Trachiniae* appears outside the intellectual range of the traditional wild horse/man, and it is unthinkable that Chiron would have behaved in so ungentlemanly a manner.

Sophocles has allowed few unkind words to be uttered about Nessus, and in one speech our sympathies may even be drawn to the beast who "suffered with the sharp point in his side" (ll. 681–82). Except when Heracles is railing against Centaurs (ll. 1095–96), neutral terms are used to describe Nessus and his assault upon Deianira. For instance, Deianira says that the Centaur touched her with *mataiai* hands. The lexicon defines *mataios* as "rash" and "irreverent," but also as "empty" and "vain." It is the same word, in fact, which Deianira uses in reference to her own actions when she hopes that carrying out the Centaur's instructions was not *mataion* (l. 587).

Elsewhere Nessus is called "hairy-chested" and "dark-haired" rather than the stronger epithets we might expect. Furthermore, Sophocles has omitted numerous unsavory details that could easily have entered into Deianira's account to the chorus of the aborted seduction (ll. 555–81). In a later version found in Apollodorus (*Bibliotheca* 2.7.6), Nessus instructs Deianira to make the *philtron* from a combination of his blood and the semen he had spilled on the ground. In Seneca's *Hercules Oetaeus,* which is based on the *Trachiniae,* Nessus prefaces his assault with the words, "Tu praeda nobis et coniunx eris" (l. 511).[9]

Heracles, on the other hand, is consistently characterized by bestial imagery, and almost all commentators have suggested that Sophocles has made him the double of Nessus and that Heracles also shares many qualities with the other beasts in the play, such as Achelous and the Hydra. Here, for instance, is S. M. Adams on the typical Athenian spectator at a performance of the *Trachiniae:*

> He knew that Heracles, son of Zeus, was sent into the world to deliver it from deadly monsters. To accomplish this, the son of Zeus must be both man and beast.[10]

In fact, Sophocles' Heracles possesses almost exclusively those traits of the hubristic Centaurs and few of those qualities we associate with Chiron. It is these typical Centaur characteristics of lust, impulsiveness, and treachery that bring about the deaths of both Nessus *and* Heracles, each by the other's hand. One of the most central of the many ironies of the *Trachiniae* rests on this basic similarity between Nessus and Heracles, an irony that is heightened by the key role that the gentle, self-effacing Deianira plays in the death of both hero and Centaur. It is even conceivable that Deianira finds Nessus enough like Heracles to respond to him in a trusting manner, a trait in her character that many critics have found in violation of *vraisemblance*. Sophocles has heightened the elevation of the Centaur in the *Trachiniae* by emphasizing the bestial aspect of Heracles.[11] If we wish to condemn Nessus for his lust and treachery, we must also condemn Heracles: if not, we succumb to the same anachronisms of *arete* and the old heroic code of which Sophocles was so intensely aware. This same juxtaposition of the old heroic code with the new political and social values of the fifth century pervades the *Ajax,* the play which Sophocles may have written just before or after the *Trachiniae.*[12]

Several fragments of inscriptions found on the Acropolis place the beginning of work on the Parthenon at 447. The metopes must have been begun immediately and finished early because they had to be put in place before the roof was built. Ancient accounts indicate that the metopes must have been

Detail, Parthenon metope, South 31.

placed by 442,[13] and their most striking aspect is the considerable variation from metope to metope in terms of style and craftsmanship. Gerhart Rodenwaldt argues that Phidias, who probably directed the sculptural work on the Parthenon, used the south metopes as a testing ground for his assistants—those whose works were unsatisfactory were not invited to contribute to the later work, i.e., the frieze and the pediments.[14] This weeding out of assistants would also explain the much greater homogeneity of style and expertise in the frieze and pediments.

The most archaic of the metopes is South 31 in which, according to Rodenwaldt, the face of the Centaur resembles a grotesque theater mask.[15] This particular metope was surely done by an older or very conservative artist who was still operating with the artistic principles of the previous generation and who was not asked to continue working on the Parthenon sculptures.[16] There is nothing else among the surviving Parthenon sculptures like it.

However, the most grotesque Centaurs were not always created by the most conservative sculptors. A Centaur head, now in the Acropolis Museum, has been shown to belong to metope South 7, one of the most stylistically advanced.[17] The face here, although hardly comparable to that of South 31, has the kind of lines and creases we associate with the Olympia sculptures. Similarly, the Centaur of South 29 has a large animal's ear, yet the maiden he carries is draped in the same Mature Classical style as the Iris of the west pediment.[18]

Of the twenty-one Parthenon metopes in which Centaurs appear, the most interesting—for our purposes—are South 4 and South 30. The most remarkable is South 30, which has what appears to be an expression of pity on the face of the elderly Centaur. Of this metope Rodenwaldt has asked the rhetorical question, "In the Parthenon era, was a motif conceivable in which the Centaur might for a moment be stopped by a feeling of sympathy with the youthful antagonist?"[19] But it is in South 4 that we see a face whose serene expression is practically interchangeable with that of the youth. This head, located in Copenhagen, could be "the portrait of a handsome, refined gentleman in the prime of life."[20]

All that separates the Centaur's face in South 4 from those of the youth's is his beard—for the Greeks of this time a sign of barbarism. But consider the drawing of the Centaur in South 27 by Carrey, the Frenchman who sketched all the Parthenon

Centaur head from Parthenon metope, South 4.

Detail, Parthenon metope, South 30.

sculptures prior to the bombardment of 1687. The beast in this, by most accounts, most Classical of metopes is beardless.[21] Unfortunately, the metope Carrey actually saw in 1674 is now irretrievably without a Centaur head. If Carrey did indeed correctly copy a beardless Centaur, and if its features were as completely human as the Centaur in South 4, that other Mature Classical composition,[22] we would see represented here the final step in the process of humanizing the Centaur that is documented on the Parthenon metopes. Brommer, however, insists that all the Parthenon Centaurs were bearded and that Carrey falsely restored a head that was missing when he drew the metope.[23] Brommer supports his case against Carrey's reliability with reference to several distortions which he finds in the drawings.[24] None of Brommer's contentions are, in my opinion, completely valid, and certainly none of the distortions he points to are of such a magnitude as to make us suspect that Carrey would go so far as to draw a head where there was none. It is especially difficult to believe that Carrey could have beheld a row of metopes with twenty-one consistently bearded Centaurs and then sketched in one beardless head on a Centaur.

My thesis would be of little matter if it stood or fell on the basis of one beard. The noble visages of the Centaurs in South 4 and 30, and probably in 27 and 28,[25] for which we only have the sketches by Carrey, are consistent with the new ideas that we associate with the Mature Classical period of Periclean Athens. No longer do grotesque monsters hubristically attack the civilized Greeks while Apollo urges on his favorites. The program, whether by intention or not, does not allow such clarity of meaning along the south side of the Parthenon. If the centauromachy of the metopes was meant to suggest the Persian Wars to Athenians, it was in an entirely different spirit than the centauromachies of a generation earlier. On the metopes, when a youth and a Centaur are portrayed in conflict, more often than not the beast has the upper hand. Perhaps for the Greeks of Phidias's time Centaurs were more than allegorical representations of Persians and the "barbarians" of the non-Greek world. Perhaps Centaurs came to symbolize that necessary Dionysian counterpart to the Apollonian impulse which directs so much of the architectural and sculptural ideas of the Parthenon. This signification was always inherent in the mythical tradition, in the *nomos/physis* dichotomy of the two classes of Centaurs, but it was never so carefully worked out in the fifth century as in the sequence of the south metopes.

It is likely that the *Trachiniae* and the Parthenon metopes date to the same five-year period in fifth-century Athens, and it is certain that the Centaurs of the *Trachiniae* and the Parthenon are substantially more humanized than those in the earlier works of Pindar and the Olympia sculptors. However, this comparison can be enhanced by our contention that Sophocles departed from tradition by emphasizing the bestial qualities of Heracles and by making Deianira a completely sympathetic character. Both of these changes are typically Sophoclean—they deepen the tragic resonance of the drama. It is also likely that Sophocles has invented Nessus's stratagem of the *philtron* and created a new tradition. There is no extant work in art or literature prior to Sophocles that portrays Nessus as so fully developed. Regardless of the actual source or sources from which Sophocles worked, he has appropriated the Centaur in a totally novel way. If we knew more about the meaning of the south metopes of the Parthenon,[26] we could better extend our comparison with the *Trachiniae*. I do think, however, that it is safe to say that the source for the south metopes originally conceived of the Centaurs as something less than noble.

The new attitudes of the 440s that the *Trachiniae* and the south metopes reflect have their roots in the fascination with balance which we find in the art of the Mature Classical period. T. B. L. Webster has found the definition of Classicism in the perfect balance between realism and form; he also explains its downfall:

> When under the influence of new thinkers passion becomes more important than modesty and cleverness than wisdom, the two components, realism and formalism, are developed to the jeopardy of the whole.[27]

Webster's remarks on Classicism and the impact of the Sophists on Athens in the 440s suggest a rationale for the balance that Sophocles achieves between Heracles and Nessus and the corresponding balance that exists between the youths and the Centaurs on the Parthenon metopes. It may also help explain the change from the Early Classical works of Pindar and the Olympia sculptors to the Mature Classical works. Although the earlier artists forcefully endorsed the virtue of *sophrosyne*—the opposite of hubris—they violated it in a way that they never suspected. In the next generation, *sophrosyne* is extended not only to the meaning of the work, but in a sense, to the execution of the work. In spite of the fundamental chauvinism of the Parthenon's program, a certain modesty stops the Mature Classical artist from even so trivial an act of pride as portraying his fellow humans as superior to a Centaur.

The wisdom, modesty, and prudence of the glorious Athens of Pericles' funeral oration are frequently cited to explain this kind of phenomemon. However, there was a darker side of this wisdom that figures strongly in Classical art. In the years after the rout of the Persians, the Athenians could see themselves as militarily and morally *kallinikoi,* of noble victory. However, as Athenians began to have increasingly bitter differences with their former Greek allies in the years that followed, and as the Sophists worked at clouding traditional Greek values, the *kallinikos* ideal began to fade. Factions became more polarized, and the meaning of the previous generation's victories became ambiguous. The clear-cut ideas of good and evil in 479 were obscured in the years of jockeying for power with Sparta and more or less lost by the time of the Peloponnesian War: the flawed heroes of Sophocles in the 440s (Heracles, Ajax) are midway between the god-fearing Orestes of Aeschylus and the morally delinquent Orestes of Euripides.

As the notion of a *kallinikos* ideal was losing its validity for Athens, and as the memory of Salamis and Plataea was subsiding with time, the myth of the centauromachy was stripped of much of its previous force. Although it was still capable of attracting the likes of Phidias in the years just after 450, we can see how he and his coworkers transformed it. The dignified, victorious Centaurs of the metopes can no longer allegorically represent the barbaric, hubristic Persians. If they have anything at all to do with Athens's former antagonists, they represent the Persians as Herodotus portrayed them during this same period, as a passionate, hardy, wine-loving, nature-worshiping people.[28] Greek artists show a more sophisticated understanding of symbolism as Centaurs become the embodiment of an equally serious part of the human spirit—one we have called Dionysian—which the Greeks of this time were beginning to place alongside its more traditional virtues of order and moderation. The Sophists—good or bad—cannot be discounted here, for it was they who argued for giving full rein to the passions. The extremes that were associated with Centaurs were no longer denied their position in the human mind, and we may wish to associate this change of attitude with subsequent Athenian history: Athens's behavior in the years to come was not a model of moderation in all things. At any rate, Sophocles' Nessus cannot be regarded as an allegorical Persian either. He is a creature of passion, and like the Parthenon Centaurs, an ennobled one.

Unlike Pindar and the Olympia sculptors who show the Centaurs as grotesque intruders in a world of virtuous heroes and their Olympian sponsors, Sophocles and the Parthenon sculptors give us Centaurs with many more human qualities. The Centaurs of the later generation are capable of more thought and feeling—Nessus can devise a clever scheme, and at least two of the Parthenon Centaurs seem almost gentlemanly. The Centaurs of Sophocles and the Parthenon sculptors are not the forces of barbarism fighting hopelessly against civilized Greeks—Nessus is not unlike the passionate, impulsive Heracles whom he eventually defeats, and the Parthenon Centaurs appear to be gaining the upper hand more often than not. Finally, the Centaurs of the 440s are not clearly "unhonored either among men or amid the ordinances of the gods" (*Pythian* 2.43). No Apollo urges on the Parthenon youths as at Olympia, and in the *Trachiniae* there may not even be an apotheosis for Nessus's victim, Heracles.[29] The reworking of a mythical type—the humanizing of the Centaur—is part of the cultural history of a society that moved from its halcyon days at the end of one war to the brink of another war as tragic as a play of Sophocles.[30]

Notes

1. Paul V. C. Baur, *Centaurs in Ancient Art: The Archaic Period* (Berlin: Curtius, 1912), p. 3.

2. G. S. Kirk, *Myth: Its Meaning and Functions in Ancient and Other Cultures* (Cambridge: Cambridge University Press, 1970), p. 157. See also Kirk's *The Nature of Greek Myths* (Woodstock, N.Y.: Overlook Press, 1974), but cf. Alex Scobie, "The Origins of 'Centaurs,'" *Folklore* 89 (1978): 142–47, esp. p. 145.

3. Ibid., p. 160. It is surprising that Lévi-Strauss has never discussed Centaurs, especially since there is an explicit distinction between the eating of raw and cooked meat in one of the Centaur myths. Page duBois, in "On Horse/Men, Amazons, and Endogamy," *Arethusa* 12 (1979): 35–49, has used the work of Lévi-Strauss to support her thesis that Centaurs, by nature opposed to marriage, reveal by contrast "the ways in which marriage is used in Greek thought as a model for culture itself" (p. 35).

4. T. B. L. Webster, *Greek Art and Literature 530–400 B.C.* (London: Oxford University Press, 1939), p. 55. For recent scholarship on the mural, see John P. Barron, "New Light on Old Walls: The Murals of the Theseion," *Journal of Hellenic Studies* 92 (1972): 20–45.

5. See the excellent photographs in Bernard Ashmole and Nicholas Yalouris, *Olympia: The Sculptures of the Temple of Zeus* (London: Phaidon, 1967).

6. C. M. Bowra, *Pindar* (Oxford: Clarendon Press, 1964), p. 410. All translations of Pindar are my own.

7. Although history has given us firm dates for the Parthenon sculptures, there is no hard evidence for the date of the *Trachiniae.* I agree with Earp, Schwinge, Reinhardt, and Kamerbeek that the play was writen prior to Euripides' *Alcestis* of 438. Furthermore, I agree with Gordon M. Kirkwood who, in the appendix to his *A Study of Sophoclean Drama* (Ithaca, N.Y.: Cornell University Press, 1958), places the *Trachiniae* between the *Ajax* (447) and the *Antigone* (442). This is precisely the same period during which the Centaur metopes were sculpted. It would not be too extreme to suggest that Sophocles contemplated Centaurs while watching the sculptors in Phidias's workshop. For the most recent speculation on dating the *Trachiniae,* as well as a good bibliography on the matter, see T. F. Hoey, "The Date of the *Trachiniae,*" *Phoenix* 33 (1979): 210–32.

8. It is not likely that a Heracles legend which united Deianira with Nessus's philtron and Iole predated the *Trachiniae.* Works by several authors have been suggested as sources for the *Trachiniae,* but we know so little about them that the question becomes almost meaningless. A concise account of the possible sources for the *Trachiniae* can be found in J. C. Kamerbeek, *The Plays of Sophocles. Commentaries Part II: The Trachiniae* (Leiden: Brill, 1970), pp. 1–7, although some of what he says has been made obsolete by the discovery of a fragment of Hesiod's *Eoiae.* It is available in *Fragmenta Hesiodea,* ed. R. Merkelbach and M. L. West (London: Oxford University Press, 1967), pp. 15f. , and it tells us that Deianira acted with "great recklessness" when she handed over a poisoned *chiton* to Lichas, who then delivered it to Heracles. However, we still do not know Deianira's motivation, nor can we be sure that the *pharmakon* was given to her by Nessus in Hesiod's version. Indeed, we have no hard evidence in literature or in art that Heracles killed Nessus with a bowshot prior to the presentation of the *Trachiniae,* and consequently we cannot suppose that Nessus could have exercised his stratagem on Deianira during or after the time Heracles applied the sword to him. In Dithyramb 16 of Bacchylides, ed. Bruno Snell (Leipzig: Teubner, 1970), Iole, Deianira, Nessus, and his "divine gift" are united as in the *Trachiniae,* but this dithyramb was almost certainly composed after the *Trachiniae.* The minority view in the matter of Sophocles' originality is expressed by Charles Dugas in his "La Mort du centaure Nessos," *Revue des études anciennes* 44 (1943): 21ff. Dugas has found a fragment from a sixth century vase that could show Heracles attacking with sword in hand a Centaur who has *already* been pierced by an arrow in the neck. From this and from the non-Sophoclean accounts in Diodorus Siculus and Apollodorus, Dugas argues that Sophocles adopted a rare old tradition in which Nessus has time to give instructions to Deianira.

9. For a fuller comparison of the *Trachiniae* with Seneca's *Hercules Oetaeus,* see Gunnar Carlsson, "Le Personnage de Déjanire chez Sénèque et chez Sophocle," *Eranos* 45 (1947): 59–77. Other Latin works can be cited to further illustrate Sophocles' restraint in handling Nessus. Ovid (*Metamorphoses* 9.101) and Seneca (l. 507) both attach the adjective *ferox* to the Centaur. Lucan (6.392) uses *improbus,* and Martial (9.65) calls the philter *perfidia dona.* Compare these with the largely neutral terms we find in the *Trachiniae.*

10. S. M. Adams, *Sophocles the Playwright* (Toronto: University of Toronto Press, 1957), p. 108.

11. Until very recently the majority opinion among Sophoclean scholars ran against Heracles: "It is generally agreed that Heracles is an unsympathetic character in the *Trachiniae.*" J. H. Kells in *Classical Review* n.s. 12 (1962): 185n. However, this opinion has recently been disputed by Charles Segal, who must now be considered the definitive interpreter of the *Trachiniae.* See his three recent studies: "Sophocles' *Trachiniae:* Myth, Poetry, and Heroic Values," *Yale Classical Studies* 25 (1977): 99–158; "Mariage et sacrifice dans les *Trachiniennes* de Sophocle," *L'Antiquité classique* 44 (1975): 30–53; and the chapter in *Tragedy and Civilization: An Interpretation of Sophocles,* Martin Classical Lectures, vol. 26 (Cambridge, Mass.: Harvard University Press, 1981), pp. 60–108. With his usual acuity and scrupulous attention to Sophocles' imagery, Segal has made several connections between Heracles and Nessus. See "Sophocles' *Trachiniae,*" pp. 106f. and 109. However, Segal also argues that Heracles' emerging heroism at the end of the play has been too strongly denied by other critics (pp. 130ff.).

12. See Bernard M. W. Knox, "The *Ajax* of Sophocles," *Harvard Studies in Classical Philology* 65 (1961): 1–37.

13. Bernard Ashmole, *Architect and Sculptor in Classical Greece* (New York: New York University Press, 1972), pp. 95f. That the metopes were executed between 447 and 442 is fairly certain. For a survey of critical opinion, see Frank Brommer, *Die Metopen des Parthenon. Textband* (Mainz: Zabern, 1967), p. 174. Extensive photographs of all the Parthenon metopes can be found in the companion volume.

14. Gerhart Rodenwaldt, "Köpfe von den Südmetopen des Parthenon," *Abhandlungen der deutschen Akademie der Wissenschaften zu Berlin* 7 (1948): 5. Translations of quotations from this essential essay are my own.

15. Ibid., p. 18.

16. Brommer, *Die Metopen,* p. 127.

17. A. H. Smith, *The Sculptures of the Parthenon* (London: British Museum, 1910), p. 3.

18. Brommer, *Die Metopen,* p. 123.

19. Rodenwaldt, "Köpfe von den Südmetopen," p. 16.

20. Ibid., p. 17.

21. Brommer, *Die Metopen,* pp. 118ff.

22. Ibid., p. 82.

23. Ibid., pp. 228 and 117.

24. These distortions include the addition of an oak wreath to the Centaur head in South 9 (*Die Metopen,* p. 227), the depiction of a scroll in South 20, which now exists only in fragments (ibid., p. 227), and the poor rendering of the proportions of a head in South 16, now also in fragments (ibid., p. 100). It is entirely likely that an oak wreath, whether of organic or imperishable material, could have been placed in the bore holes in the head of South 9, or that the bore holes themselves could have been mistaken by Carrey, drawing from a distance, as some kind of wreath. The integrity of the fragment on which Brommer bases his premise concerning the scroll in South 20 is ambiguous, and the contention that Carrey portrayed the head in South 16 as "too broad and massive" seems to me a red herring—there are many inexact but faithful renderings in Carrey's drawings that Brommer might just as easily have mentioned. Carrey's drawings are collected in Theodore Robert Bowie and Diether Thimme, eds., *The Carrey Drawings of the Parthenon Sculptures* (Bloomington, Ind.: Indiana University Press, 1971).

25. Rodenwaldt, "Köpfe von den Südmetopen," pp. 14f.

26. The problem rests in the unknown significance of the middle south metopes that were destroyed in the bombardment of 1687. Carrey's drawings show a series of scenes that are not consistent with any known version of the Lapith centauromachy. If the middle scenes are from some other story, we are faced with the anomaly of a row of metopes that lack the extraordinary unity of every other aspect of the Parthenon program. Brommer has suggested that the south metopes show an Attic saga, now lost, which combined certain unmistakably Attic elements with a centauromachy modeled after the Lapith wedding legend (*Die Metopen,* p. 239). As a result, Brommer has avoided calling the young men in the metopes "Lapiths." I have followed his example by referring to them as "youths." (Brommer has *Jünglinge.*)

27. Webster, *Greek Art and Literature,* p. 146.

28. Herodotus *History* 1.131–36.

29. There are two versions of the end of Heracles' mortal life. In Homer (*Iliad* 18.117) he dies the death of an ordinary mortal, but Pindar has told the story of his apotheosis and his reconciliation with his old antagonist, Hera (*Nemean Odes* 1.69–72). Many interpreters have made the case that Sophocles has suppressed the apotheosis of Heracles in the *Trachiniae* as part of his condemnation of the hero. But others have argued that there are hints in the *Trachiniae* that the apotheosis takes place *after* the final speech of Hyllus. The case for Heracles' apotheosis as well as a good bibliography on other views can be found in Segal, "Sophocles' *Trachiniae,*" pp. 138ff.

30. I owe an immense debt of gratitude to the late Diether Thimme for the ideas expressed in this paper. It was he who taught me that differences in the depictions of Centaurs can be understood in terms of changes in Greek values.

Form and Protest in Atonal Music: A Meditation on Adorno

Lucian Krukowski

Washington University

THEODOR ADORNO's view of the development of modern music is both apocalyptic and pessimistic. As a witness to the social crises of the early twentieth century, he locates analogous crises in twentieth-century music. He correlates the two through a thesis of historical discontinuity wherein "modernism" contrasts with its own—"traditional"—past in certain essential ways.[1] The evolutionary thesis of historical development is, for Adorno, inadequate sociology because the twentieth century, by and large, constitutes a betrayal of the earlier ideals of personal freedom and political equality. Equally, the thesis of formal continuity in music is inadequate aesthetics because modern music, in reaction to its own social matrix, takes on the function of criticism. The valuable work of traditional music is accounted a "master-work," which signifies a certain accessibility of the work to its social institutions through performance and appreciation. For Adorno there can be no masterpieces in twentieth-century music because the imperative of criticism or protest inhibits accessibility and fosters alienation. Thus, the valuable modern work is counted a "radical-work," one that confounds the received practices of appreciation, yet which exemplifies the most advanced historical development of musical form.[2]

One distinction between Adorno's thesis and the garden varieties of "social realism" is that Adorno tries to reconcile radical sociology and radical music and thereby challenges both purely formalist and purely instrumentalist aesthetics. For him, the value of music is to be found both in its innovational achievements and in its utility for social change, or—at least—social "witness." Radical music is seen to omit the devices of integration properly characteristic of traditional works—although improper for modern works—and the consequence is that radical music is doomed to remain largely unheard. However, Adorno does not view this as simply an unfortunate historical happenstance but rather as a deliberate artistic choice, perhaps the only choice that preserves the autonomy of musical form while it supports the stance of protest. Radical music protests precisely through its inaccessibility—its not being heard. In his analysis, Adorno's musical polemics are supported by his social polemics. My question here is essentially how the latter are exhibited in the former. In my discussion I do not analyze Adorno's sociology; I accept it as a "given" and ask only how the music he champions can be understood to exemplify his attacks on "bourgeois" society. For my thesis it does not matter whether Adorno's criticism of modern society is correct, for I wish only to indicate a link between a particular normative content and a particular musical form.

Adorno's heroes, as is well known, are Schoenberg, Berg, Webern—the principal early exponents of atonal,[3] or "dodecaphonic," music. The direct evolutionary paths to this music are found, importantly, in the preatonal, "expressionist" works of these composers and in the developments of nineteenth-century music, primarily of Beethoven, Wagner, Brahms, Mahler, with Beethoven perhaps cast as the primary exemplar of a music that, for a fleeting historical moment, is both autonomous and accessible. I shall not, here, pay much attention to Adorno's villains, Stravinsky, Hindemith, et al., nor to an analysis of what constitutes musical villainy except in the obvious sense that it involves a rejection of Adorno's tenets for musical value.

My principal aim is to locate the critical function in atonal music, i.e., where, structurally, "protest" occurs and how it is manifested. Adorno says much about this, but it remains elusive. He does not say what I eventually come to say, although I feel that he implies—at least some of—it. Adorno discusses the inaccessibility of radical music primarily in terms of its social "fate"—the dearth of performances and the indifference of audiences. But there is a problem here: the fate described is not unique to radical music; it is suffered by all obscure works—of whatever kind. More importantly, this account identifies only the negative factor of social avoidance and does not tell us what form some positive, or "correct," appreciation would take. Evidently we need to know this if we are to ascertain the fact of musical protest and come to recognize specific instances of the music at issue. My own thesis in this regard can be preliminarily stated as follows: the radical music of which Adorno speaks is inaccessible because it is inaudible. I define inaudibility as a particular relation between the twelve-tone row as it is constituted in the score, and the score as it is performed. I hold that adequate appreciation here cannot be limited to the performance but must include certain nonsensuous aspects of the score. The listener is enjoined to refer the auditory event to the notational deployment of the row. However, the requirements for such reference exceed what can be ascertained through listening and, therefore, adequate appreciation for such music presupposes data and beliefs that are come by in other ways. The protest function in radical music is to be found in this restructuring of appreciation and in the concomitant social insights it provides.

Before I proceed to develop my "inaudibility" thesis through a more detailed discussion of dodecaphonic music, I will first look at some "ordinary" uses of this term and thereby develop certain differentia between the notions of "traditional" and "radical." Common sense would indicate that for music to be appreciable it should be audible. It could thus keep good company with "visible" visual art and "legible" literature. Nothing tricky here, only the claim that the sensuous vehicle is a sufficient condition for the aesthetic experience. Music, prima facie, seems to fit this claim better than do its companions: the visual arts although sensuous, elude being "vehicles" insofar as they are nonnotational;[4] literature, on the other hand, locates its sensuousness not in the script but in the imagination. Perhaps this is what prompted Hegel to give music the middle position in Romantic art.[5]

Music, as it is both sensuous and mediated, should manifest a linkage between these two aspects. Accordingly, we consider the sounds we hear in performance to be referents of the score, although we also know that only some of the performance characteristics are specified by that reference. The reverse of this—whether we hear what is *in* the score—translates easily into a question of value: whether we *should* hear all that is written. It would seem, offhand, that if we did not hear what the score contains, either the music has failed or we did not listen closely enough. "Musical failure," here, might be taken as a matter of the composer's ineptness: a score so conceived that some of it, under accepted standards of reference and acuity, cannot be distinguished as a sound-event. However, I will argue, apropos "radical" music, that this is not to be regarded as a failure because in such music scores maintain a unique independence—both formal and valuational—from their performances.

Failure to hear can also be blamed on the performance, that some part of the score was played incorrectly, although, on some such occasion, we might like what we did hear. Correct performances of the same work differentiate by emphasizing certain aspects of the score and obscuring others so that of the aspects which are audible we only attend to some. Conductors occasionally claim (less these days) that they perform works as these were "originally" scored—or "intended." But such claims do not easily sustain belief, for they each come to be seen as another instance of one obscuring another's emphasis. So the notion of "paradigm performance" crumbles and new versions of familiar works continue to proliferate. "Radical music," however, is less susceptible to variations in performance, for its appreciation—as I claim—is not entirely vested in listening. One expected consequence of this is that such music is infrequently played. I will argue that this expectation contributes to a criticism of the music's social matrix.

Another "failure to hear" can be blamed on us—the audience. We defeat audibility in any number of ways: when we hum along as we dine, or interweave the music with images of lovers, voyages, or childhood sorrows. We may, in defense, blame the music—some works in particular—for being seductive on this score although we might also admit that resisting such seductions is a way to a more adequate appreciation. One need not hold for this view that hummable and image-invoking music must be bad, only that, if worthwhile, it invariably is historical and not autonomous in regard to social requirements of service. This suggests that modern "radical" music, as it has "finally" achieved autonomy,[6] is subject to no requirements external to its form, and it therefore teaches us to listen within earlier music for the autonomy—the formal self-sufficiency—that there remains covert.

On two counts this thesis fits well into the Hegelian framework of Adorno's aesthetics. 1) Music is placed with other social forms in the urge to historical progress, i.e., the "evolution of spirit" from external imposition to self-determination or "freedom." In this sense musical works have relative—historical—value. 2) Music is viewed through a purely internal tradition of masterworks in which the possibilities of musical form evolve but the degree to which each level of possibility is realized does not evolve. In this sense musical works have absolute value independently of their historical position. On two other counts, however, this thesis departs from its Hegelian roots. 1) In Hegel, the quest for autonomy shows a series of historical approximations. Its full achievement, while not assigned the status of a Kantian "regulatory ideal," is, nevertheless, historically remote. Adorno's construal of modern "radical" music indicates that it is now fully—and finally—free of the social impositions and requirements connected with music's contribution to other (nonmusical) social functions. 2) Within the Hegelian dialectic, a victory in the quest for autonomy implies a transformation of a form into a "higher" state. The evolutionary process thus continues, although now with a more "purified" content. Art forms achieve dominance and then fade in the course of history but each demise is also a success; it augurs a new beginning and is a cause for philosophical optimism. Adorno's construal of radical music, however, indicates that it achieves autonomy at a quite un-Hegelian price. "Success," here, does not produce a further continuity but, rather, a historical stasis and alienation. New music is not, in its turn, gracefully superseded; it is shunned.

I have thus far construed the notion of "inaudibility" as evidence either of compositional ineptness or appreciative failure. But, now, if we follow Adorno's "historical discontinuity" view of both modern art and modern society, "inaudibility" takes on a very different meaning.

Traditional music performs social service in different specific ways, e.g., through its roles in church liturgy, in expressions of nationalism, in court and salon affairs, in festivals. The inability to appreciate such music typically marks some individual deficiency, e.g., in birthright, education, wealth, religious or political persuasion. "Aesthetic appreciation," in this context, functions as an arbiter of background, taste, and influence. "Failure to appreciate" indicates an inability to understand the uses of what one hears and, by extension, to function in the social milieu for which these works were made. Such failures are not solitary affairs of the psyche; they are manifest as public behavior, for, in order to perform a discriminatory function, failures in appreciation must be noted by those who succeed. These remarks point to the alliance, in a traditional context, between the arts and social status, and to the role of the arts in the preservation of social institutions. "Appreciation," here, is in the service of the dominant social class, and its exercise serves to clarify and support rather than to undermine this class.

The role of music in contemporary culture is conceived very differently when we follow Adorno's argument. The general premise of discontinuity between modernism and the past can be specified in the late bourgeois "betrayal" of Romanticism. When Adorno refers to music as an "essentially bourgeois art"[7] he refers specifically to music from Beethoven on—that is, to music whose development parallels the rise of the Western democracies. The specific parallel is between the possibilities of social freedom and musical autonomy. The actuality, as Adorno describes it, is the failure of continuing social transformation: the failure to achieve Marxist-utopian social ideals, the ensuing degeneration of bourgeois culture, and the rise of totalitarian states. Music, in a certain sense, fares better for Adorno than society, for although the forces of conscious decadence are evident (Stravinsky, Hindemith), the trivialization of music overwhelming (Musak, "pop"), yet the achievements of Schoenberg and his group do fulfill the possibilities implicit in early Romanticism. However, as was noted earlier, this achievement has a cost. The growing disparity between social and musical development couples formal freedom with social alienation. Within its development music discards its traditional service function, yet it is unable to assume a new symbiotic relation with its culture. The social role left to music that is compatible with autonomy is the critical one. By virtue of the demands its appreciation makes upon the listener, music strives to destroy society's illusions and to present it with its actual face. This coupling of autonomy and criticism transforms new music into radical music. Further, it furnishes the value criteria that distinguish "radical" works from other new works, those that through retrograde devices, e.g., "Neoclassicism," "Mannerism," avoid the critical task.

What are these "demands of appreciation" imposed by radical music and what relation do they have to the music's formal properties?

As I have indicated, Adorno's view of musical history is at once discontinuous and apocalyptic: a formal teleology is realized and a social irrelevance is suffered. If music's formal victory is thus rendered hollow by society's indifference, adequate appreciation of such music must itself be compensatory to this indifference. It must be an act more austere, perhaps more aggressive than we have traditionally understood appreciation to be. When we view appreciation as an "enjoyable" experience, we usually presume a link between such enjoyment and certain properties of the subject, e.g., "wholeness," "harmonious articulation of parts," "satisfactory resolution of development." In this framework, the experience is counted as most desirable—perhaps most "aesthetic"—when the descriptions of its subject also serve to describe the affective state of the audience. Whatever "harmony," "wholeness," "satisfaction," are taken to mean when applied to things or events, these terms are seen as—at least—analogously descriptive of the experiences of such things or events.

But this is familiar territory so I now move directly to the hypothesis that, in general, this sense of appreciation accords primarily with those historical periods in which music has both a service and a musical function, when it is designed to ingratiate as it unfolds.[9] Inadequate appreciation, in this context, occurs when the service function is mistaken as the paramount one. It is here that Adorno finds the seeds of radical protest. Traditional music performs a *covert* criticism when its listeners succumb to the temptation of luxuriating solely in the ongoing present, when they engage in purely linear listening because they are seduced by the apparent familiarity and predictability of the harmonic and melodic sequences. Failure to resist such temptation makes for indiscriminate appreciation because what is then experienced is typical surface rather than unique structure. A more adequate appreciation of such music does not, however, entail a puritanical disavowal of enjoyment but, rather, its "going through."[10] Such deeper appreciation requires that enjoyment of sequence be coupled with "spatial" understanding, i.e., a grasp of the music's "shape," where experience of the musical event configurates across, as well as within, the flow of time. This requirement is analogous to a silent "reading" of the score where one may skip pages, return to beginnings, and preview conclusions.

But few of us—however accomplished—would wish to confine appreciation to perusals of scores. Obviously, a performance satisfies more than "music in the mind."[11] We require performances, we say, because music is "underdetermined" by its score, and we point to the constitutive nonnotational differences between performances. While this assertion is usually meant to include all music—traditional and modern—I will argue that in a special sense Adorno's "radical" music is "overdetermined" by the score and that this alters the requirements for its appreciation. But first I would like to pursue the "underdetermination" thesis a bit further.

The "service function" I take as a characteristic of traditional music is indicated, in part, by the music's accessibility, at some level of appreciation, to the most unsophisticated listener. Another indicator of traditional structure is the importance of appreciation of differences between performances. The performer can be seen here as a mediator between the "self-sufficiency" of the score and the listener's need for gratification. The performer makes the score accessible not only by giving a sensory specification of the notational elements but also by adding to them, "socializing them, with the non-scored liberties of interpretation. The continuing attractions of multiple performances of traditional music is a mainstay of our concert halls and recording industry. This, in itself, attests to the importance for the appreciation of such works, of the differences between their performances.

In listening to traditional music, we assume that all the notational properties of the score are semantic properties, specifically, that the compliant is the performance we hear. It may be exceedingly difficult in large-scale orchestral music to discriminate all atomic compliants, i.e., the individual sounds of all scored notes. But we consider these to be indirectly audible in the sense that they contribute to the sonority of the whole; we presume that their absence, upon repeated listenings, would come to be noticed.[12] We take this as a challenge to our own acuity, and also as showing distinctions between performances through relative emphases on different aspects of the score.

However, we would clearly distinguish between a deemphasized note and an unplayed note because we would want to maintain—for any correct performance—the *possibility* that every scored note can be heard. This promise of audibility places adequate appreciation entirely in the auditory event. Of course, there are other things we may want to know about the work that we find in other places, e.g., analyses, historical and biographical data, etc. But such things we count as either irrelevant to appreciation per se, or as helping us to appreciate the work by directing our attention to what there is *to* hear.

I propose now that this description of appreciation, which is appropriate to the context of traditional music, must be modified for Adorno's category of modern "radical" music because there appreciation is *not* entirely located in the auditory event. Adorno accuses his society of rejecting a dialectically feasible—historically achievable—ideal in favor of a retrogression to specialized sectarian interests. Yet this "decadent" society, in striving to project an illusion of coherence, takes as its *own* analogue the antiquarian forms of traditional music. Accordingly, its adherents reject as "meaningless" or "unenjoyable"[13] the modes of experience that would be adequate to the forms of new—radical—music. While radical music exemplifies the furthest evolution of musical form, its social matrix testifies to a historical failure. It is this failure that a successful appreciation of radical music purports to reveal.

A more detailed account of radical form and its appreciation is now needed. Adorno indicates that between the received array of syntactic elements—the "system" of notation—and the procedure of composing lies another procedure: the choice and design of a twelve-tone row. He describes this design as "a preliminary study by the composer . . . before the actual composition begins," and continues: "Music becomes the result of processes to which the materials of music have been subjected and the perception of which in themselves is blocked by the music." He says further that "the compositional process actually begins only when the ordering of the twelve tones is established."[14] The choice of a row, then, is not arbitrary, but nevertheless is an activity distinct from the composition of a particular piece. The "same" row may underlie a number of different compositions, yet the musical work, once complete, includes both the formulated row and the composed piece upon which it is based. The strictures of the row upon the piece are, by now, familiar, e.g., the requirement that every tone of the row be sounded in sequence before any can be returned to. Adorno points out that use of the row may be extremely complex and rich, each version allowing for a number of variants and their derivations within a given composition.[15] The elaboration of a row into its variants—unlike the choice of row itself—need not occur prior to composition, but, nevertheless, each variant is linked through a logical derivation to the original row. The rigor of this derivation, as with the design of the row, is independent of the compositional activity where the row and its variants are deployed. I observe here that the formulation of the row and the derivations of its variants are musical but not auditory events in that they are not retrievable from the performed piece. More precisely, these "logical" events are aspects of the syntax of the work that do not have auditory compliants in the work as sound-event.

Adorno describes dodecaphonic (consistently twelve-tone) music as polyphonic in structure. This indicates that each horizontal sequence is a particular exposition of a chosen row, but no exposition is modified for the sake of the character of the vertical clusters, i.e., the "chords" that are formed by the parallel nature of these sequences. In the hierarchic structure of traditional harmony, elements differ in both structural and auditory value. Not all elements are part of coherent horizontal developments; some arise in particular places simply as contributions to the sonority of a vertical, chordal progression. That such elements may not individually be audible seems perfectly in accord with their "service function," which is the support and elaboration of the principal themes.

In modern polyphony, however, there are no "principal themes"; Adorno denies that there are any themes at all.[16] All horizontal sequences are self-sufficient, and each musical element is autonomous in that it functions primarily in the development of the sequence to which it belongs. This presumption of autonomy rests, of course, on the rule that the occurrence of a note is justified not primarily by reference to sensibility but by its place in the exposition of a row. Sensibility is not, thereby, rendered obsolete in this type of music, but its exercise is contingent upon the compatibility of any given choice with the systematic nature of the row.

If music conceived in this way were located entirely in the sound-event, one would expect the greatest transparency in texture so that each element of each row could be precisely heard. One would also expect the greatest clarity in shape so that the exposition of each row could be followed in its entirety. Such expectations would arise from our knowledge of the importance given, in the music's underlying theory, to the rules governing the use of the row.

Yet, we know that in paradigm examples of atonal music these expectations are often not met. In some works, multiple sequences develop simultaneously, and the dynamics of their orchestration create dense textures in which the identities of particular notes are masked. In other works, the expositions of rows occur in vastly different time frames, some in quick runs that are on the extreme edge of distinctness, others in prolonged passages that undermine the span of attention. In still other works, the variations on a row may be so numerous and complexly stated that they escape identification, and consequently, the shape of their exposition is not perceived.[17]

When we consider these and other auditory characteristics of dodecaphonic works, we find a disjunction between performance and score that seems willful in its thoroughness. The works resist the impression of unity and completeness even upon repeated hearings. The consistency in the projection of fragmentary and discontinuous sound clusters does not, however, permit any evocation of playfulness or randomness. To the contrary, it suggests a seriousness that seems all the more immutable through its resistance to our listening. So we are led to assume a rigor that is located outside the sound-event, one that *no* performance or accumulation of performances can reveal. If we do assume this, then, in general, we understand the critical nature of this music: a protest made by its withdrawal from its sound. But, in particular, we realize that "appreciation," here, encompasses two distinct events, neither of which is subsumable to the other. One event is independent knowledge of the rule-conditioned properties that specify the score; the other is listening to the performed work. "Nonsubsumable" is important here, for it provides the distinction between traditional and radical music in this regard. "The "service function" of traditional music appropriates the score into itself. A score is a professional matter, a part of the procedures through which performances are generated but not in itself a thing for appreciation. Although we may use a score to inform and enhance our listening, the relevant properties are the auditory ones and the proper subject for appreciation is the performed music. As I noted earlier, the appreciation that correlates with traditional music identifies "enjoyment"—however "disinterested"—as its end. As privileged recipient of this "end," the listener need not recursively attend to the means as a condition of enjoyment, for the means, i.e., the composing and performing functions, are end-directed. They provide the adequacy of the performed music for the appreciative act.

In the atonal music Adorno champions, however, the relationship between score and performance is not one where the score is subsumable as a means to appreciation; the score, rather, is a *subject for* appreciation. As such, it shares the appreciative act with the performance. I believe that this dual requirement for the appreciation of radical music underlays Adorno's conception of the dual function of the musical work itself: it exemplifies formal progress as regards the history of music, and it projects criticism of the society within which the music is composed. In such a society, one could argue, the use of traditional music contributes to the illusion that all is well. The satisfactions of harmonic development appropriate to another time are taken—inaccurately—as analogues of the social dynamics of our own time. The enjoyment we find in listening and the self-sufficiency of the concert experience encourage us to apply the same strategies of encapsulation to our dealings with the world. Thus habituated to the equating of appreciation and pleasure, we find the experience of atonal music disconcerting, and we may either reject it or mistake it. We reject it if we do not enjoy its sound, and we mistake it if we "manage" to enjoy its sound. In the first case we reject what we hear because it lacks the harmonic predictability to which we are accustomed; in the second case we accept the sound object because we are willing to extend our enjoyment to the apparently chaotic and discontinuous. But in both cases we make our judgments on the basis of listening alone. Adorno remarks that in modern music, where the service function is no longer present, the work is in danger of being taken as an ornament, a mere thing.[18] The paradox here is that appreciation is inadequate whether, in missing the illusion we need, we reject what we hear, or in contenting ourselves with surface, we come to enjoy what we hear.

In atonal music the score exhibits the unconditioned nature of the row. It is unconditioned in the Kantian sense that it is freely taken on but then functions as a binding rule. Fidelity to this rule is a concern that is independent of the concern for the row's exposition through its auditory compliants—the performed sounds. Indeed, the inadequacy of performance in projecting the rule-governed structure of the row serves as a *reproach* to those who are content to "merely listen." The nonaccessibility of atonal music functions critically in that it identifies the listener's failure to recognize the music's conceptual nature. This failure is seen as a symptom of the more general failure to recognize the nature of society and the need for social transformation.

Adorno construes the dialectic of musical development apocalyptically in that he sees it as having stopped, as being frozen in the extremes of its last antithesis—between "gestures of shock" and a "crystalline standstill."[19] In the expressive content of radical music, "passions are no longer simulated, but rather, genuine emotions of the unconscious—of shock, of trauma—are registered without disguise."[20] "Formal ossification" is to be interpreted as the "negation of the severity of life."[21] If we go along with Adorno's claim that music is concerned with "truth,"[22] then the truth in radical music is not a pleasant one. About the "general listening public," Adorno remarks, "the dissonances which horrify them testify to their own conditions; for that reason alone do they find them unbearable."[23] The inability to hear the sounds as music makes them unbearable, but then few can identify the form of appreciation that would make them music, and those few *already* understand the nature of the protest involved. Adorno's polarization of dialectical extremes, e.g., between "crystal" and "shock," also shows up in his distinction, within radical music, between "expressionist" and "objective" works. In one sense all radical music is "expressionist" in that its "truth" is obsessed with the ravages of the human psyche. In another sense "expressionism" represents the last historical stage of incomplete atonality, where vestiges of traditional form strain to preserve the music's accessibility for the general listener and thus render its expressive content both palpable and consequential.[24] In this second sense, "objective music" is seen as the move away from the "thesis" of expression into the "antithesis" of indifference. Adorno says of Schoenberg's late works that they "pose again the question of content regarding subject matter, without pretending to achieve the organic unity of this content with purely musical procedures."[25] Elsewhere he states: "Dissonances arose as the expression of tension, contradiction, and pain. They (now) take on fixed contours and become 'material.' They are no longer the media of subjective expression. For this reason, however, they by no means deny their origin. They become characters of objective protest."[26] But there is a problem here, for I noted above that Adorno considered the greatest threat to "New Objectivity" to be the possibility of its interpretation as "ornament." How, then, does expression that becomes fixed as "material" retain the power of protest? How does such acoustic material escape being identified as merely decorative sound and, thus, not consequentially symbolic at all?

The attribution of "objectivity" to completely atonal works is surely supported by the systematic nature of the twelve-tone row. But if the row, as I suggest, is not thoroughly articulate in—cannot be retrieved from—the sound, the listener's volition to include the scored row in appreciation must be located elsewhere. This volition undoubtedly begins with an awareness of the music's context: the social and personal circumstances of its creation. But it proceeds through an incorporation of context into content by relocating these circumstances *in* the work. It concludes by relocating the work itself. As Adorno points out, the typical categories through which we distinguish appreciative ability, e.g., "layman," "connoisseur," "expert," are of little use here, for these categories are formed within the very institutions against which radical music protests.[27]

The formal intransigence of the row correlates well with the seriousness of the protest. While use of the row does not preclude sensibility, it is not primarily governed by the appeal to sympathetic distributions of sound. Appreciation in atonal music, then, cannot take as its primary function a progressive sensitivity to the quality of such distributions in performance. I have indicated that the historical development of radical music is marked by failure in social accessibility. If we now define "social accessibility" as a situating of appreciation in performance, we can hypothesize that "musical protest" entails using the performance as a referent to something extraneous to it, something nonauditory which nevertheless completes and gives specific identity to the auditory. The imperatives that formed radical music necessitated relinquishing many characteristics of traditional music. These characteristics are not, as such, irreconcilable with atonality; e.g., the row can, in fact, be used to generate harmonic vertical progressions. But the retention of such characteristics—the pursuit of sympathetic sound—produces a contemporary lie: the exaltation of feelings that accord with willful illusion, not actuality.[28] In the expressionist phase of radical music the feelings projected are authentic, but they become increasingly hard to bear; they are fixed at their extremes. Reality is made more painful by the betrayal of hope: the failure of nineteenth-century social ideology in the situations of the twentieth. In his analysis of Expressionism, Adorno speaks a good deal of "loneliness"; he also speaks of "impotence." The sexual metaphors here are illuminating: "loneliness" entails a yearning for the contact that brings self-completion; "impotence" entails the inability to assuage loneliness through action. One way of coping with the pain can be found in play, in a retreat to illusion where other identities supplant or replace one's own. But in music Adorno sees this as a corruption of integrity, a historical recidivism that he rejects. Another way out is through a forced indifference to feeling, through an autodissection where feelings lose their interconnectedness in organic subjective experience and are reconstituted in abstract arrays. Here even the desire for accessibility is relinquished, yet for Adorno this constitutes progress: another historical veil has been pulled aside and the value of what remains has been affirmed. On this score he states: "Expressionism was not sufficiently radical in its position on superstitions regarding the organic . . . the elimination of the organic resulted in a new crystallization of the concept of the work of art; the works necessarily became heirs to the expressionist heritage."[29]

Traditional music—from which Expressionism is not totally emancipated—is characterized by Adorno as "unified" or "hermetic" in structure, which unity, in turn, is based upon the "identity of subject and object." Objective music, on the other hand, he characterizes as "fragmentary," lacking in unity, and because of this "transformed into protest."[30] This bears directly on my thesis of the nonauditory aspect of atonal music. In traditional music, the composer's identity—better, intentionality—is transformed into a universalized model in which private individual feelings are replaced by generalized, intersubjectively recognizable, "modes" of feeling. This is a way of affirming the thesis that music contains within itself the subjective content of its making, and is therefore independent, as regards its meaning, from considerations of the maker or composer. But this thesis, in turn, is based upon the assumption that the musical form presents itself as a basic analogue to the form of subjective experience. The experience of the work is meaningful independently of reference to other experience precisely because it is fundamentally like that other experience. In this regard Adorno quotes Benjamin's characterization of "hermetic" as "uninterrupted sympathy of the parts with the whole."[31] Of course, the supposition that such an analogue occurs would technically require the posit of an underlying "parent" structure by reference to which the claims of similarity or analogy could be justified. Failing this, one could theorize, as I believe Adorno does, that this thesis of structural commonality between "art and experience"[32] is a historically delimited one which is tenable only so long as neither aspect is found wanting. The "hermetic" nature of art, then, is not music's essential characterization but only marks a historical stage, one which is now over. As "experience" falls prey to nostalgia and self-deception, "art" relinquishes the formal characteristics that would support the analogue. Radical art thus becomes hostile to traditional art, and "through hostility to art, the work of art approaches knowledge."[33] In radical art, enjoyment is replaced by "perception," specifically, a perception of the music's "lack of unity" and thus—from the traditional standpoint—its "meaninglessness." But art that "approaches knowledge" cannot, at the same time, lack meaning.

In traditional music, meaning is found in performance because it is there that music presents itself, ruminates on its own development, and completes itself. Appreciation follows along and nothing more is needed. In radical music, listening identifies formal fragmentation, a nonhermetic structure that thwarts the sense of completeness. The frustration attendant on seaching for the musical work in its performance is what Adorno calls "meaninglessness." This is, perhaps, an infelicitous phrase, but it must be understood in a specific way: the experience of "meaninglessness" identifies the music's function as protest. The inadequacy of the performed sound of radical music for the needs of an appreciation appropriate to traditional music is not a lack; it is an admonition. It warns against a more serious inadequacy: a perception of the world by the listener such that the traditional forms of meaning would still be wanted.

Yet, radical music must be rescued as music, for random sound can also properly be experienced as "fragmented." But the "meaninglessness" of random sound could not maintain the seriousness of protest, that seriousness which forces another interpretation and expands meaninglessness into knowledge. The completeness of radical music is not an arbitrary imposition effected by the listener; it is in the work. It is in that aspect which connects the sound fragments to a source that is irreproachably coherent: the row in notation. Although this coherence may not be heard, it can be known, and the inclusion of such knowledge in appreciation changes the face of the art. It provides Adorno's distinction between "traditional" and "modern" in music by identifying those works which are authentically—or "radically"—modern.

These days, the designation "modern" is a catalyst for extended rethinking about the nature of historical change in the arts and, correspondingly, about how we define and assess works of art. Our notion of modernity is now "bracketed," and having thereby lost its role as designator of present practices, has become historical. This notion now identifies the period, only just past, that we have come to call "modernism." My discussion here has largely been about one concern that is characteristic of this period: artistic form and social theory joined under the concept of "transcendence." Interpreting Adorno, I have proposed that we construe certain artworks as entities which join theoretical and physical aspects in their ontology[34] and thereby function as social instruments as well as formal exemplars. The postscript that suggests itself is the question as to how Adorno's particular thesis has fared over time—the time of transition into the period sometimes identified as "postmodernism." Does "Adorno-Schoenberg" remain an adequate theoretical support for a music whose ambition, after all, is to persevere in its claim of greatness? Does Schoenberg need "rescuing" from Adorno's "failed" sociology? Only a few comments are possible at this point: we cannot suppose that Schoenberg "rid of" Adorno is Schoenberg "plain," only Schoenberg rethought. If it is the case, as I have suggested above, that interpretations may be counted as proper parts of artworks, then it should follow that we can assess them aesthetically. Under this assumption Adorno has a chance: at the least, his thesis has intensity, scope, elegance, and, importantly, goes beyond the limits of "mere" (Adorno would say "bourgeois") sensibility. To be sure, we cannot stay with Adorno; he is too pointed, too preoccupied with old wounds. But he conceives of art as crucial in a sense that we will be hard put to match.

Notes

1. The text this commentary focuses on is Adorno's *The Philosophy of Modern Music.* Although an early text, I believe it to be germinal in the formulation of his ideas on the development of music and the "crisis" of modernism. The tensions of his subject are mirrored in his style: assertions given are immediately taken away and turned on their backs. This has been criticized as "jargon"; it can be defended as "nonsuppression of antagonisms," a virtue usually assigned to the free operation of a social dialectic. Either way, Adorno is an easy target for criticism of an analytic sort. But he is, after all, a major theorist of modern art, a period of especial interest to us now that, from all accounts, it is over. If one is concerned with the art, it seems to me more important to circle about the underlying beliefs than to spear them straight away for their inconsistencies, arrogances, or whatever. This is probably what Heidegger meant by "understanding," and it seems a good way to understand Adorno.

2. The "modern-traditional" dichotomy now seems oversimplified if not completely untenable. Although Adorno uses it he takes pains to trace the—purely musical—continuity of nineteenth- and twentieth-century musical style. Yet there seems no doubt that he considers "true modern"—dodecaphonic—music to be functionally of a different sort than its predecessors. As my purpose here is not to challenge this thesis but to trace some of its implications, I adopt this classification in my discussion. "Traditional" music in Adorno's usage refers primarily to classical and romantic music—the music of developing bourgeois cultures. Baroque music is somewhat separate; its social context is that of autocracy, and in musical form, e.g., polyphony, it correlates more directly with modern music. Adorno divides modern music uncompromisingly between "radical" and "decadent." Such composers as Mahler and Trenek are transitional in his account to the major atonal composers: Schoenberg, Berg, and Webern. I do not comment here on Adorno's later involvement with such contemporaries as Stockhausen, Cage, and Boulez.

3. The term *atonal* can be misleading because, in a strict sense, all music is "tonal," i.e., is an array of "tones." Adorno uses the term to distinguish between music based upon the diatonic scale and music utilizing the twelve-tone row: "dodecaphonic" music. I follow this usage here.

4. The reference here is to Nelson Goodman's analysis in his *Languages of Art* (Indianapolis, Ind.: Bobbs-Merrill, 1968), chap. 4.

5. Hegel, *Aesthetics,* trans. T. M. Knox (Oxford: Clarendon Press, 1975).

6. A characteristic of much modernist theory, e.g., as found in the writings of Apollinaire, Kandinsky, and Mondrian, is that art has achieved a "plateau" of self-sufficiency which is the culmination of a historical development. Further development, on this account, entails the discovery and elaboration of possibilities inherent in this historical achievement but not a striving for further emancipation, the assumption being that there are—finally—no longer any restrictions.

7. Theodor W. Adorno, *Philosophy of Modern Music,* trans. Anne G. Mitchell and Wesley V. Blomster (New York: Seabury Press, 1973), p. 130.

8. Monroe Beardsley theorizes much in this way.

9. "Ingratiation," as an auxiliary function of music, can be correlated with the characteristic of "professionalism," i.e., the composer undertaking a task identified by the larger society as a desirable and needed one. The late-romantic and modern turn to "self-expression" or "newness" as justifications for music making, undermines the notion of "professionalism" by discarding the criterion of social desirability. Adorno reinstates this criterion through his thesis of music's critical function. But, here, the perception of criticism as a social need does not issue from the society in question but from a group alienated from it.

10. In Plato's *Phaedrus* the lover "goes through" the attractions of physical beauty in order to advance to an appreciation of formal beauty. In this aspect of Plato sensual enjoyment is seen as revelatory rather than as inhibitory to the understanding of higher virtues. This is what is at issue here.

11. This argues against Collingwood's view on the matter.

12. In *Languages of Art* Goodman makes the claim that differences between an original work and a "look-alike" forgery will eventually come to be noticed if one continues to look. Here, the importance of undiscerned notes in the context of traditional music is accounted for in a similar way. In both accounts, the possibility of eventual *sensory* discrimination is the consequent value for appreciation. I claim here, apropos atonal music, that *non*discrimination constitutes a value.

13. Adorno, *Philosophy of Modern Music,* p. 84.

14. Ibid., p. 61.

15. Ibid., pp. 62, 63.

16. Ibid., p. 59.

17. To substantiate these claims, I enlisted the help of some composer friends who were willing to lead me through an analysis of four works: Schoenberg's Third Quartet, opus 30, and his Variations for Orchestra, opus 31; Webern's Piano Variations, opus 27, and his String Quartet, opus 28. I chose these works because Adorno's frequent references to them in *Philosophy of Modern Music* point to the notion of an inherent tension between row construction and sound; see pp. 73–74, with footnote, 83–84, 92, and 109–12. While a measure-by-measure analysis is impractical here, I suggest that some support for my claims would be found in one.

18. Adorno, *Philosophy of Modern Music,* p. 70.

19. Ibid., p. 42.

20. Ibid., p. 39.

21. Ibid., p. 43.

22. Ibid., p. 4.

23. Ibid., p. 9.

24. The examples here would be of such "transitional" composers as Mahler and Krenek as well as much of Berg's work, e.g., *Wozzeck,* and such early work of Schoenberg as *Erwartung.*

25. Adorno, *Philosophy of Modern Music,* p. 20.

26. Ibid., p. 86.

27. Ibid., p. 27.

28. Adorno levels this accusation at Stravinsky and Hindemith, among others.

29. Adorno, *Philosophy of Modern Music,* p. 51.

30. Ibid., pp. 124–27.

31. Ibid., p. 125n.

32. The phrase "art and experience" refers, of course, to John Dewey's book of that name. Dewey insists on a "public" aesthetic entity that is comprised of *both* the physical work and the experiences of it. In this refusal to give primacy to the epistemological

problem, Dewey shows his debt to Hegel. Adorno would not disagree with the desirability of Dewey's program; he would consider it a historical casualty.

33. Adorno, *Philosophy of Modern Music,* p. 124.

34. I have discussed this point in some detail in my article "Artworks That End and Objects That Endure," *Journal of Aesthetics and Art Criticism* 40, no. 2 (Winter 1981): 187–97.

Literature and Society

"That Hive of Subtlety": "Benito Cereno" as Critique of Ideology

James H. Kavanagh

Princeton University

> It is with fiction as with religion: it should present another world, and yet one to which we feel the tie.
>
> —Melville, *The Confidence Man*

IT is worth remembering that critical approval of Herman Melville was belated and sporadic. Until well into the twentieth century, the dominant appraisal of Melville was set by scholars like Parrington, who found him to be a minor figure on the whole—a writer who happened to achieve an eccentric tour de force in *Moby Dick,* while groping his way from frivolous South-Sea romances to fragmented and barely comprehensible cynicism in works like *Pierre.*[1] Only after World War II did the short fiction of the 1852–56 period gain widespread critical acceptance, and then only with sharp disagreement over the relative success of the various stories. In a comment on *Pierre,* one of Melville's contemporary reviewers explicitly addressed the sore point in the post-*Moby Dick* fiction:

> We can afford Melville full license to do what he likes with "Omoo" and its inhabitants: it is only when he presumes to thrust his tragic *Fantocinni* upon us, as representatives of our own race, that we feel compelled to turn our critical Aegis upon him and freeze him into

silence . . . he strikes with an impious, though, happily, weak hand at the very foundations of our society. . . .

Let him continue, then, if he must write, his pleasant sea and island tales. We will always be happy to hear Mr. Melville discourse about savages.[2]

If George Washington Peck's criticism can be taken as paradigmatic of a critical strategy that consigned Melville to a rather severe literary oblivion,[3] the twentieth century has seen quite a change in the dominant appraisal of Melville's literary "value"—a transformation from the "eccentric" to the "aesthetic" aptly signified, for example, by the Yale University Library's reclassification (circa 1930) of *Moby Dick* from "Cetology" to "American Literature."[4] Peck's practice of literary criticism at least marks itself explicitly as judging the text's "literary" value according to whether its effects are permissible within the limits of a given ideological "reality"; his criticism can only construct the "Herman Melville" of the late fiction as unacceptable for a "literary" canon whose task it is to ratify that sense of coherent self and social order constituting a dominant mid-nineteenth-century bourgeois perception of the "real." A more flexible modern criticism has generated new paradigmatic readings of Melville's entire corpus.[5] Even a text like "Benito Cereno," itself readable as operating a critical irony against a representative of "our own race" and civilization, can be recuperated and made safe for that civilization's new ideological and literary-ideological values.

F. O. Matthiessen, the influential and progressive critic of the American Renaissance, set the terms of a mid-twentieth-century paradigmatic reading of "Benito Cereno":

In "Benito Cereno" . . . the embodiment of good in the pale Spanish captain and of evil in the mutinied African crew, though pictorially and theatrically effective, was unfortunate in raising unanswered questions. Although the Negroes were savagely vindictive and drove a terror of blackness into Cereno's heart, the fact remains that they were slaves and that evil had thus originally been done to them. Melville's failure to reckon with this fact within the limits of the narrative makes its tragedy, for all its prolonged suspense, comparatively superficial.[6]

Leslie Fiedler also found "Benito Cereno" unable to comprehend the oppressive reality of black slavery, thus ratifying the metamorphosis of a Melville whom a conservative Peck found too critical into a Melville whom a liberal criticism now understands as not critical enough:

> Captain Amasa Delano fails to recognize the rebellion on a Spanish slave ship which he encounters, precisely because he is a good American. He is endowed, that is to say, with an "undistrustful good nature" and will not credit "the imputation of malign evil in man". . . .
>
> . . . Though the fact of slavery, out of which all the violence and deceit aboard the Spanish ship had been bred, remains a part of his own democratic world as well as Don Benito's aristocratic one, Amaso Delano is undismayed. . . . Indeed, Melville seems to share the bafflement of his American protagonist; a Northerner like Captain Delano, Melville finds the problem of slavery and the Negro a little exotic, a gothic horror in an almost theatrical sense of the word.[7]

With "Benito Cereno," the paradigmatic modern critical strategy seems to have focused on the text's irony and ambiguity, promoting readings of the text as allegorizing the failure of innocence and perception—with Babo and the slaves representing a "terror of blackness" whose pervasive "Gothic horror" the "good American" (Delano) in his unfortunate "naiveté" fails to perceive, even as he is enmeshed in its complex layers of violence and deception. More subtle elaborations construe the text as leading the reader into an infinite maze of moral and epistemological uncertainty, allegorizing the story as a "paradigm of the secret ambiguity of appearances." These constructions are then implicitly ratified by recourse to Melville's own sense of cynicism, doubt, and confusion in a world unsure of its God or its truth.[8] Such readings, therefore, give us a "Benito Cereno" and a "Herman Melville" signifying the sophisticated doubt and ambivalence now acceptable in a literary canon redefined in those existential-humanist-liberal terms that constitute a mid-twentieth-century bourgeois self-perception.

We confront, then, contradictory paradigmatic readings of a literary "Herman Melville," along with another, carefully marginalized, set of what we might call insurgent readings, also appealing for their justification to an anterior "Herman Melville" as the locus of a coherent, now radical or even revolutionary, "ideology" (as "set of ideas") prior to and represented *just as it is* in the text.[9] One would not attribute such serious differences to discrepancies in intellectual perception among critical readers, nor even to discrepancies in the quantity or quality of the "evidence" available. Indeed, *every* reading can be, and is, ratified by constructing for itself, as a necessary effect of its own procedures, the appropriate "real" Herman Melville, the anterior "reality" that guarantees it. It seems appropriate to reflect on what makes possible such a heterogeneous field of literary-critical discourse in order carefully to place our own work in relation to it.

The discrepant readings of Melville, and of "Benito Cereno," I should contend, are determined more by the assumptions and intentions of modern critical readers than by those of Herman Melville in 1856. The modern reader's relation to this text is different from Herman Melville's, constructed by different historical and ideological determinations; its adequacy cannot be judged by its *proximity* to Melville's opinions, but by the force with which it operates theoretical investigations whose assumptions and purposes Melville cannot be asked to ratify. The question of what Melville was trying to promote in writing "Benito Cereno" is entirely different from the question of what the modern critic tries to promote in reading it, and the investigation of Melville's ideological opinions takes place on an entirely different terrain from an ideological analysis, or reading, of the text. It is not as if Melville's authorial work involved simply *transferring,* as it was, an anterior ideological formation from one place (the "real") to another (the "text," now implicitly "unreal"); rather, this work involved *putting into production* general, literary, and authorial ideologies, producing a specifically differentiated ideological formation *that was not there before.*[10] This difference should be especially clear with Melville, who constantly complained (as noted below) about the pressures that prevented him from presenting his ideas even "in the form" he preferred; in a more general sense, this difference is a necessary structural effect of the real, transformative labor involved in the production of any literary text as a gesture that evokes a reader's constitutive projection of meaning.

"Benito Cereno" presents a particular difficulty because it does not remain a "discourse about savages," about the primitive "terror of blackness" they supposedly represent, and that the "good American" in his naiveté fails to perceive. It becomes, rather, a discourse that both embodies and ironizes the "civilized" mind itself, as produced by a specific social formation: the "straight-thinking" Yankee mind with whose image our culture is so familiar. In this sense, "Benito Cereno" can be read as a discourse about *discourse,* about how such a mind *talks to itself,* giving itself the "evidence" with which to "perceive" and "feel" its own ruthless brand of savagery as "innocence" and "moral simplicity."[11] "Benito Cereno" appears, then, as a text that takes at once as its form of presentation and object of critique the peculiar preconscious mechanism—ideology—that allows one to imagine one's relation to the world in such a way as to "feel" *comfortable* (i.e., fully *justified*) about oneself, even while one is actively working to reproduce repressive social relations.

The word *ideology* as used in this essay does not primarily signify a consciously articulated "set of ideas" (political or other), but rather a matrix of presuppositional image-concepts that construct for one a "reality" overdetermined by imaginary investments—a formation that tenaciously resists being made conscious or explicit. Ideological "ideas" are important, but secondary, elaborations in "consciousness" of the already-unconsciously-formed "lived relation to the real" that is ideology; ideology structures "seeing" and "feeling" before it structures "thinking," and in such a way that it will never itself be seen, felt, or thought of *as* ideology, but only as the *natural* way of perceiving "the real."[12] Ideology, in this sense, is given not primarily in speeches or proclamations, but in apparatuses and practices (including those of literature and literary criticism) that persistently form those held within them into agents who tend spontaneously to articulate structures of feeling *and* sets of ideas *perfectly adequate* (even when seemingly oppositional to a given political regime) to the reproduction of a given set of class relations.

Literature, then, is a specific form of linguistic and symbolic practice that puts at stake not just opinions or sets of ideas, but these whole modes of imaging, living, and feeling the "reality" of a self and a social universe. It is as "lived relations to the real" that literature puts "ideologies" into play; literary work disassembles ideologies, even if only to reassemble, reproduce, or reinvest them with new force, breaking them from their former "natural" reality, if only to renaturalize them—but always "fixing" and displaying them on the stage of the text, usually as the lived experiences of individuals, such that they can be seen, "felt," questioned, and (possibly) understood, specifically *as* ideologies (depending on how one's theoretical gaze allows such an analysis).[13] Melville's textualizing work, for example, transforms raw materials from the "real" Amaso Delano's *Narrative of Voyages and Travels,*[14] "fixing" and displaying its ideological discourse through specifically literary modes of irony, characterization, allusion, suspense, etcetera; this work has its own effectivity, presenting the reader with the quasi-real literary story that evokes his/her own constitutive projections of perspective, dimensionality, and meaning into the text in ways determined (more or less unconsciously) by the reader's own relation to a dominant ideology, or "lived relation to the real" (including a literary ideology). Melville's literary work, then, like any other labor process, transforms his ideological raw materials, including Delano's *Narrative,* and his own ideological intentions, according to that work's own—specifically literary—demands;[15] these demands are themselves shaped by a dominant literary ideology, and must be accommodated if the text is to appear as compellingly "literary" and "real." An author *always* presents an ideology, and always *presents* it. Whether s/he wants to present it sympathetically or critically, s/he must first present it in a form that has literary "veracity." That the author must traverse this "gap" with a transformative labor is evident in the fact that, as Marx and Engels were quick to recognize, a "good" ideology does not automatically make for "good" literary production.[16]

"Benito Cereno," then, is produced under this double demand, effecting what Althusser calls an "internal distantiation" of an ideology, displaying a dominant "lived relation to the real" within itself as the lived experience of a fictional character (Delano) in a form that opens it to "sight" and analysis. This internal distancing is an objective, structural effect of the conditions of its literary production, and opens possibilities of analysis beyond any authorial intention, as irrefutably evidenced by the continuing history of such analyses. "Benito Cereno" has been a particularly controversial text for which to produce a critical reading because it insinuates the reader so thoroughly into its internal distiatation of an ideology, requiring us "to 'perceive' . . . *from the inside,* by an *internal distance,* the ideology in which it is held."[17] Thus, the text makes itself available for readings that reproduce the ideology in which Delano is held, even while explicitly criticizing him; such readings follow those "clues" of his textual discourse that tend toward metaphysical speculation, sliding over to rest on the very ideological presuppositions supporting the discourse in the same movement that generates a "corrected" or critical ironic reading of the character as too "naive" or "good-natured." But "Benito Cereno's" internal distantiation is such as to support a more acute "anti-ideological" reading of the text's structural intention, a reading that breaks definitively from the ideology that holds Delano, Melville, and in some sense all the text's readers.

"Benito Cereno," like many other Melville texts, accomplishes this internal distantiation through the formal mechanism of an ironic narration, which establishes at once the "lived experience" of, and the "internal distance" from, a specific ideological "lived relation to the real." Melville's peculiar third-person, determinate point of view, quasi-stream-of-consciousness narration ironizes the "real" Amasa Delano's discourse from the *Narrative* with subtle, often minute, syntactical changes and framing devices; this narration, then, *is* Melville's textualizing of the ideology, allowing the reader *either* to identify with the ideological "experience" of the fictionalized American Captain, or to take a critical distance from it. The reader can, and indeed must (up to a point), live in the experience and perception given by Delano's fictional "consciousness," which dominates the bulk of the text; yet, in maintaining the difference between Delano's "eye" and the text's "I," the text also allows the reader to see, this time as an object, "the way Delano sees." Indeed, that same *écriture* of long complex-compound sentences, within which Delano tries forever to bury the knowledge of his real activities within social relations, can become for the critical reader a map with which to extricate one's self from Delano's ideological maze and discover his displayed but denied repressive political role. This extrication seems to require two readings, since the reader is usually "deceived" along with Delano on first reading;[18] the second reading must be not just a rereading of the text, but a reading of one's own first reading, of one's first spontaneous relation to the text and to the ideology it puts into production—a reading that can indicate how the preconscious ideological matrix in which the reader is held (the "shifts and side-slippings" of even the twentieth-century reader's "ordinary consciousness")[19] is enough like that of Amasa Delano that one can be "fooled" into identifying with his "deception." By making one "follow the leader" through the immanent critique of Delano's ideology, the text brings one up against the complex of violence and death that is its repressed "end" and allows one to make a break from it.

This formal subtlety can be read as textualizing a previous ideology of Melville's in the sense that it sublimates his own contradictory *relation to* (not his "ideas about") the prevailing ideological sense of self and reality persistently reproduced by the system of social relations and literary practices in which he lived and worked. Melville, along with his contemporaries, certainly "bathed" in an ideology much like that of Amasa Delano. That he knew, or at least "saw" this somewhat differently did not mean he could escape it, and his literary practice was formed under its pressure. He lived this contradiction so acutely that the implicit force of this ideology, inherent in the apparatuses and practices of literary production, became for him an explicit form of censorship, as real and oppressive as that operated by any commissar: "Dollars damn me," he wrote to Hawthorne. "What I feel most moved to write, that is banned—it will not pay. Yet, altogether, write the *other* way I cannot."[20]

While we do not claim that Melville would specify the "what" and "that" of his complaint with the same theoretical terms that will supply our reading of his text, it seems clear that Melville was working at once to conceal and preserve a radical distance from dominant general and literary ideologies. That a Melville text might be using a vocabulary of "bachelors and maids," "Captains and sailors," "whiteness and blackness" indirectly to critique the liberal ideology accompanying mid-nineteenth-century American class practices, in a way that eludes an effective ideological censorship, seems to have been somewhat more difficult for American literary criticism to perceive, and to comment upon forcefully, than analogous indirections in foreign texts produced under political censorship.[21] But there are many ways of being "frozen into silence." The ironic characterization of Delano in "Benito Cereno," then, can be read as an imaginary working-up of Melville's own lived contradiction precisely in its determinate (critical) "fixing" of this paralysis, of the inability to remain at ease within, or get definitively out of, an oppressive ideology.

In an important sense, then, "Benito Cereno" is an ambiguous text because it has to be; its indeterminacy of meaning is real and forced, an objective reality, insofar as the text is a materialization of an impossible lived contradiction, whose precise ideological significance Melville cannot supply. This textual ambiguity derives from a contradiction internal to the work of an author working within/against bourgeois ideological practices, an author whose implication in those practices prevents the formulation of critique, save as double-edged irony or "anti-literary" silence. But *this* "ambiguity" is a structural fact of the text, constituted for knowledge by a theoretical investigation of how this, or any other text, functions; it is by no means a (let alone *the*) substantive theme or *meaning* of the text, something which can only be given by an operation of reading, governed by different purposes. In reading, one supplies meaning to the text, constructing significance from the play of its "differences" in ways determined by one's relation to contemporary ideologies. To supply a meaning in terms of "ambiguity of appearances" has no a priori precedence over supplying one in terms of an "unambiguous critique of ideology" (as this paper will attempt), and receives no particular sanction from the recognition in other terms of the text's structural "ambiguity"; the same word appears here, but in two entirely different problematics.

It should be clear that this theoretical placement of the literary text is far from what is usually understood by any New-Critical autonomization of the "text itself."[22] Indeed, I intend to suggest that the text has *no* "meaning" except as a specific instantiation of a set of relations, including relations to dominant literary and general ideologies. The history of the text is nothing but the history of such instantiations, resulting from its successive entrance into changing literary and literary-critical practices. This reading of "Benito Cereno," like all others cited, is an attempt at a transformative instantiation or enactment of this text, which inscribes it in new relations to dominant literary and general ideologies, and makes it effectively available for a certain form of teaching practice. The critical reading of "Benito Cereno" that follows presents a way of reading the text which encourages certain specific meanings and excludes others, as a critical reading of this type must do. The rationale for any such reading derives not from Melville, nor from the "text itself," but from a criticism's own implicit or explicit intention to resolve in some specific way the struggle over which ideologically significant meanings will be given the support of a text now recognized as having literary "value" and aesthetic "power." The "validity" of such a reading rests primarily in how comprehensively and persuasively it puts the text into production for these purposes. Far from "autonomizing" text or criticism, this view forces the critical reader to take full responsibility for understanding as carefully as possible how his/her work contributes to reproducing or challenging a dominant ideology, for consciously operating the appropriate theoretical and rhetorical strategy to intervene in that profoundly political, unceasing, and unavoidable struggle over the meaning of words, and of those peculiarly effective word-systems we call literary texts.

In this reading of "Benito Cereno," everything hinges on the character of that irony which is the text's internal construction of a distance from a dominant ideology. The analysis of "Benito Cereno" must begin by breaking absolutely the seductive grip of "identification" between the reader and Amasa Delano, a grip not even loosened by the seemingly negative judgments of the American Captain carried in phrases like "moral simplicity" and "weak-wittedness."[23] Indeed, such a language remains perfectly consistent with Delano's own form of self-understanding—as pretense of critique that actually absolves him of all responsibility. Criticism must not meander unwittingly in the metaphysical fog of Delano's internal discourse, but must dispel it. A criticism that takes the grammar of Delano's ideological self-consciousness as its own is bound to reproduce his strategy of evasion through perplexity. Thus, one must insist that the "gap" which the text installs as its ironic critical distance from Delano cannot be interrogated solely as an epistemological problem of knowledge and ignorance, but must also be sharply posed in terms of an active responsibility within a set of social relations.

One should not have to belabor the text's careful internal historical framing of events. We can surely read as significant the text's setting of this story of a rebellion in 1799, a period flush with the triumphant victories of the American and French Revolutions, a period whose "momentousness," as Melville elsewhere remarks, is unexceeded "by any other era of which there is record."[24] These victories promised the establishment of a new social and political order whose ideological promise of "liberty, equality, fraternity" (or "life, liberty, and the pursuit of happiness") was held out as the rational, democratic replacement for the decadence and superstition of feudal societies, as the "rectification of the Old World's hereditary wrongs"[25]—of which no country provided a more regressive example than Spain. The tension between the American and Spanish captains is heavily laden with these contrasts, as is made explicit in Delano's condescending, moralizing judgment of the "Spanish spite" that he thinks impels Cereno to punish Babo: "Ah," Delano sighs, "this slavery breeds ugly passions in man.—Poor fellow!"[26]

And this story was written, of course, in 1855, at a time when the hypocrisy of precisely that liberal democratic ideology had just been challenged (in Europe if not in America) by the revolutions of 1848—at a time, therefore, when the violent and repressive tendencies of liberal ideology itself were now visible (including even the restoration of monarchist political forms for the purposes of bourgeois reaction). In the United States at this time, the commercial and legal institution of chattel slavery that still served as a material underpinning of capitalist democracy was coming under direct attack in incidents like the *Amistad* rebellion—incidents that shook Northerners as well as Southerners.[27]

This is the frame in which one must read Captain Delano's inability to understand what he sees aboard the *San Dominick*. It is in this frame that one must register the deep, bitter irony with which the narration follows the intricate contours of Delano's mind, a mind the text describes as itself "incapable of satire or irony" (p.75). There is no such thing as "ideology in general," and this text does not take as its object just any ideology, but the specific form of bourgeois ideology exuding from the social relations of the most "advanced" sectors of the most "progressive" bourgeois society. At stake in this text is not the "problem of evil" as figured in the blacks, nor the problem of precapitalist forms of social relations as figured in Cereno and Aranda, but the problem of ideology as figured in Delano; at stake is how a man like Delano—neither a decadent aristocrat, nor even a Southern slaveholding American, but precisely a "Northerner" from the most radical and abolitionist of states (Massachusetts)—can think of himself as liberal, progressive, and charitable while staring in the face of his own racism, paranoia, and authoritarianism. At issue in "Benito Cereno" is how, for a man immersed in Delano's ideology, a belief in one's own "goodness" and "moral simplicity" is not just "naiveté," but a necessary condition for the violent, sometimes vicious, defense of privilege, power, and self-image.

Such deliberately sharp conclusions can be supported by a careful reading of how the text's ironic narration superimposes what Delano thinks and says over what he *does*. It is a mistake—it is *the* mistake—to read this text for the ambiguous knowledge it gives at any moment of "events aboard the San Dominick"; one must rather read the text for the unambiguous knowledge it gives at every moment about Delano's ideological construction of, and self-insertion into, that situation. The text becomes eminently readable once we assume *that* as what it intends to communicate. As is generally recognized, the ironic stance toward Delano is quickly and firmly established with his initial reaction to the sight of the *San Dominick:*

> To Captain Delano's surprise, the stranger, viewed through the glass, showed no colors; though to do so was the custom among peaceful seamen of all nations. . . . Captain Delano's surprise might have deepened into some uneasiness had he not been a person of a singularly undistrustful nature, not liable . . . to indulge in personal alarms, any way involving the imputation of malign evil in man. Whether, in view of what humanity is capable, such a trait implies, along with a benevolent heart, more than ordinary quickness and accuracy of intellectual perception, may be left to the wise to determine. [P. 55]

The ironic distance established here from Delano's perceptions is more extreme than one would expect from a character with whom the text supposedly "identifies" more strongly than others, whose "bafflement" Melville "seems to share." With the last sentence of this paragraph, the text makes Delano an object of criticism bordering on derision, saying definitely, if indirectly, that he is stupid. Nor is the moral virtue of his "undistrustful good nature" unambiguously ratified by the text. Many critics take this phrase at face value as the text's explicit definition of Delano's "problem," but I should claim that the sentence can be read with the "whether" governing the clause about a "benevolent heart," as well as that concerning Delano's "intellectual perception," leaving it uncertain "whether . . . such a trait implies . . . a benevolent heart."[28] Thus, the *écriture* of the text begins on this first page of the story as a complicated discourse of formal *politesse* and deference to Delano, a discourse that actually squirrels away—conceals *and* preserves—radically negative judgments about him. The reader might "feel" that s/he has read something positive about Delano in this sentence ("benevolent heart"), but the one characterization most clearly communicated is: "Delano is thick-headed." This characteristically Melvillean prose makes the text "difficult" for many readers and "flawed" for many critics, but it is not some kind of fault that can be dispensed with; it is a necessary condition of a textual production that distantiates an ideology within the discourse of that ideology itself.

Indeed, criticism has at times pondered Delano's "bafflement" with an *esprit de sérieux* similar to his, often ignoring passages where the text is unmistakably *comic,* dissolving Delano's sense of self-importance by making him a butt of its humor. In the scene, for example, where the "not unbewildered" Delano falls through the *San Dominick*'s railing, a reader with the least pictorial imagination might find it difficult to keep from laughing *at* Delano:

> As with some eagerness he bent forward . . . the balustrade gave way before him like charcoal. Had he not clutched an outreaching rope he would have fallen into the sea. The crash, though feeble, and the fall, though hollow, of the rotten fragments, must have been overheard. He glanced up. With sober curiosity peering down upon him was one of the old oakum-pickers. [P. 89]

And in the scene when an old sailor surreptitiously hands Delano a knotted rope, the text characterizes Delano's reaction with withering irony: "For a moment, knot in hand, and knot in head, Captain Delano stood mute" (p. 91). A critical reading should treat Delano's "bafflement" as he cannot treat the knot: "Undo it. Cut it. Quick." Otherwise, like him, it will prevent itself from seeing what *is* serious: in this instance, the fact that the old man's life is at stake.[29]

Given this kind of textual ridicule, which occurs as Delano cogitates on Cereno's puzzling behavior, it would seem consistent to find the text framing his imaginings of Cereno with equally severe irony. And, indeed, in his rumination the reader finds a Delano shifting in a schizophrenic pattern from a belief that everyone is conspiring to kill him to a satisfied certainty that everyone loves him too much to do him any harm. The following passage can be read as a kind of case study in megalomania, paranoia, and racism:

> From something suddenly suggested by the man's air, the mad idea now darted into Captain Delano's mind, that Don Benito's plea of indisposition, in withdrawing below, was but a pretense: that he was engaged there maturing his plot, of which the sailor by some means

> gaining an inkling had a mind to warn the stranger against; incited, it may be, by gratitude for a kind word on first boarding the ship. Was it from foreseeing some possible interference like this, that Don Benito had, beforehand, given such bad character of his sailors, while praising the negroes; though, indeed, the former seemed as docile as the latter the contrary? The whites, too, by nature, were the shrewder race. A man with some evil design, would he not be likely to speak well of that stupidity which was blind to his depravity, and malign that intelligence from which it might not be hidden? Not unlikely, perhaps. But if the whites had dark secrets concerning Don Benito, could then Don Benito be any way in complicity with the blacks? But they were too stupid. Besides, who ever heard of a white so far a renegade as to apostatize from his very species almost, by leaguing in against it with negroes? These difficulties recalled former ones. Lost in their maze, Captain Delano . . . had now regained the deck. [Pp. 89–90]

With this passage, one can give a truly "symptomatic" reading of Delano:[30] megalomania—Delano feels that he is at the center of everyone's attention, not because of what he has done or might do, but because of what he *is;* thus, Delano thinks that the lowly sailor risks his own life to save Delano out of "gratitude for a kind word"; paranoia—everyone, under the control of the mirror-image figure of authority (Cereno), is plotting against him, plotting to take away *his* power; racism—Delano puts every possible construction on the evidence before him except the correct and most obvious one, and this possibility he refuses to consider because the blacks are "too stupid."

Delano's misrecognition here exemplifies the "overdetermination of the real by the imaginary" in ideology.[31] There is a real enough sense in which Delano is the center of everyone's attention and in mortal danger, but this sense is not congruent with the "reality" he "perceives." Delano "sees" as "real" only the situation that conforms to his imaginary struggle with his sole "equal" in rank, race, class, power, and therefore (for Delano) intelligence—Cereno. Cereno functions as a kind of mirror for Delano in the text: the similarity of their names, and their tendency always to confront each other face-to-face suggest Cereno's "imag-inary" status. The puzzle of Cereno, then, becomes the puzzle of what Delano sees in his own mirror, how it reflects his own image back to him; and Delano sees many disturbing things: arbitrary cruelty, decadence, weak-mindedness, etc. But most disturbing, he sees his own ultimate vulnerability, an image that seems to be dissolving before his eyes—a nightmare image for Delano indeed. Delano wants

Cereno to be a mirror in which his own image of power and security is confirmed and justified, and when Cereno fails to play that role appropriately, Delano then "sees" him as a figure of evil, plotting against Delano's own power.

The character of Delano, then, can be read as a textual figure of an ideology in crisis. For Delano, the crux of the problem is to reconstruct a confirming "reality" of power and authority—the "natural" authority of racial superiors (whites), and the political authority of social superiors (Captains, "gentlemen"). The whole scene aboard the *San Dominick* appears as unsettlingly "unreal" to Delano because it presents an image of social power relations that lacks the appropriate materials for any "reality" he can construct. Thus, Delano's anxieties center on loss of control—either his possible loss of the *Bachelor's Delight,* or his perception of Cereno's loss of control of the *San Dominick;* what most confuses Delano about the scene aboard the *San Dominick* is the absence of the network of repressive practices and apparatuses that would ratify his own heavily imaginary sense of himself and of reality, that would reproduce the ideology (the "lived relation to the real") which would make his world *look* as it should:

> At bottom it was Don Benito's reserve which displeased him. . . . So that to have beheld this undemonstrative invalid gliding about, apathetic and mute, no landsman could have dreamed that in him was lodged a dictatorship beyond which, while at sea, there was no earthly appeal. . . .
>
> . . . Some prominent breaches, not only of discipline but of decency, were observed. These Captain Delano could not but ascribe, in the main, to the absence of those subordinate deck-officers to whom, along with higher duties, is intrusted what may be styled the police department of a populous ship. [Pp. 63–64][32]

What most calms Delano, then, is the image of restored authority, an image that alternates between the megalomaniac project of restoring the "weak" Cereno to his command, and the paranoid project of heading off the "evil" Cereno's plot against Delano's own command. The text makes explicit Delano's imaginary version of aid to the foreigner as counterplot:

> Evidently, for the present, the man [Cereno] was not fit to be intrusted with the ship. On some benevolent plea withdrawing the command from him, Captain Delano would yet have to send her to Conception, in charge of his second mate. . . .

> Such were the American's thoughts. They were tranquilizing. There was a difference between the idea of Don Benito's darkly pre-ordaining Captain Delano's fate, and Captain Delano's lightly arranging Don Benito's. [P. 83]

In this story about the suppression of a revolt off the coast of Chile, can modern criticism read the text as sharing Delano's self-serving idea of this "difference"? We shall see how Delano goes about "lightly arranging" the fate of the *San Dominick.*

Given the text's consistently critical and ironic "fixing" of Delano, notions of "moral simplicity," or of a "bafflement . . . Melville seems to share" with his "good American" protagonist about "the problem of slavery and the Negro" seem entirely inadequate to describe how the text presents a Delano who muses thus:

> There is something about the negro which, in a peculiar way, fits him for avocations about one's person. Most negroes are natural valets and hair-dressers; taking to the comb and brush congenially as to the castinets, and flourishing them apparently with almost equal satisfaction. There is, too, a smooth tact about them in this employment, with a marvellous, noiseless, gliding briskness, not ungraceful in its way, singularly pleasing to behold, and still more so to be the manipulated subject of. And above all is the great gift of good-humor. Not the mere grin or laugh is here meant. Those were unsuitable. But a certain easy cheerfulness, harmonious in every glance and gesture; as though God had set the whole negro to some pleasant tune.
>
> When to this is added the docility arising from the unaspiring contentment of a limited mind, and that susceptibility of blind attachment sometimes inhering in indisputable inferiors, one readily perceives why those hypochondriacs, Johnson and Byron—it may be, something like the hypochondriac Benito Cereno—took to their hearts, almost to the exclusion of the entire white race, their serving men, the negroes, Barber and Fletcher. But if there be that in the negro which exempts him from the inflicted sourness of the morbid or cynical mind, how, in his most prepossessing aspects, must he appear to a benevolent one? Captain Delano's nature was not only benign, but familiarly and humorously so. At home, he had often taken rare satisfaction in sitting in his door, watching some free man of color at work or play. If on a voyage he chanced to have a black sailor, invariably he was on chatty and half-gamesome terms with him. In fact, like most men with a good, blithe heart, Captain Delano took to negroes, not philanthropically, but genially, just as other men to Newfoundland dogs. [Pp. 99–100]

The text certainly "knows" what is going on here.[33] The critical reader knows, even if s/he did not on *first* reading, that

Delano is himself the "manipulated subject of" a rebellious black man threatening to slit his captive white master's throat. With this assumption, it is impossible to read this text as identifying with Delano's ideological perception of the blacks; it is impossible not to read this text as fixing for a scathing ironic gaze the preconscious mind-set of a character whose ignorance of his own mortal danger derives precisely from his assumption that blacks can be treated and *seen* as "Newfoundland dogs." Nor, again, is there any reason to assume that more irony falls on the way an ideological discourse constructs Babo's "limited mind" than on the way it constructs Delano's "benevolent one." The text, furthermore, painstakingly frames in this scene, as sharing the attitudes of paternalism and condescension toward blacks, two pillars of English literary culture—Johnson and Byron. This scene, then, unites in a unique literary tableau the Spanish aristocrat, the liberal-minded American Yankee, and the Tory and "revolutionary" literati—diverse instantiations of general and literary ideologies—under the sign of shared delusions about "inferior" people, about servitude, power, and the security of privilege.[34] All of these men remain unable, literally, to *see* the reality of the hatred and incipient rebellion that stares them in the face because ideology constructs for them a "reality" upon which their eyes (and their "I"s) can rest with comfort, finding a reassuring reflection of their own essential innocence and self-satisfaction.

It would be no less ideologically "skewed" to read this scene in any other way, and certainly to read it as anything like a symptom of "Melville's failure to reckon with the injustice of slavery within the limits of the narrative [which] makes its tragedy . . . comparatively superficial."[35] "Benito Cereno" can be read this way only from within an ideology similar to that signified by the text's evocation of Johnson, Byron, and Amasa Delano; the text can be read this way, that is, only from within a lived relation to a literary "real" that would limit the range of possible meanings for this text of a "great American author" in the same way as Delano's ideology limited his perception of the possible meanings of "Don Benito's" actions aboard the *San Dominick*—an ideology that would make it impossible to conceive that Melville's text might be so radically "in complicity with the blacks." Such a discourse finds in every possible meaning of this text ratification of its own image of the world, of literature, and of itself: either Melville is to be slapped on the wrist for being a little racist and corrected with a moderate dose of liberal humanism, or he is to be congratulated for showing us once again (what all "great literature" shows us) that evil and ambiguity are everywhere, if only we would see them, and that the only (regrettably imperfect) choice an intelligent person can make is for the "benevolent" and "genial" mind itself. Such a critical ideology hardly imagines that this text might be read "with" the blacks, nor even that it might be read irrevocably *against* the "good American," let alone that reading it might rudely force the reader to choose between accepting or refusing Delano's ideological "lived relation to the real," "undistrustful good nature" and all. In my view, Melville's narrative gives the reader just this choice, just this opportunity, with a force equal to that of any modern theoretical critique of ideology.

Lest the reader register the paternalism of Delano's ideology as referring only to "inferior" *races,* the text describes Delano's thrill at the sight of his own sailors approaching in the small boat:

> The sensation here experienced, after at first relieving his uneasiness, with unforeseen efficacy soon began to remove it. The less distant sight of that well-known boat—showing it, not as before, half-blended with the haze, but with outline defined, so that its individuality, like a man's, was manifest; that boat, *Rover* by name, which, though now in strange seas, had often pressed the beach of Captain Delano's home, and brought to its threshold for repairs, had familiarly lain there, as a Newfoundland dog; the sight of that household boat evoked a thousand trustful associations, which, contrasted with previous suspicions, filled him not only with lightsome confidence, but somehow with half humorous self-reproaches at his former lack of it. [Pp. 91–92]

Ideology is precisely that network of "a thousand trustful associations" upon which Delano seizes with glee at the sight of his boat. The boat and the associations it evokes are singularly comforting reminders of the relationships of power and authority that encode the social universe of a man like Delano, and secure his position as "master," this time over social inferiors of his own race but of a different class, to be treated as well with the condescension and paternalism normally reserved for a "Newfoundland dog." And the simple textual movement of the set-off adjectival phrase, "like a man's," indicates with subtle but definite emphasis that, for someone immersed in Delano's ideology, every man's individuality functions as a reminder of his own power. Indeed, so inflated is Delano with the impending verification of the natural social order promised by the arrival of "his men," that he virtually dissolves in regression, assuring himself that nobody can hurt him because he is innocent (Who accuses him? Of what?) and God watches over him:

> "What I, Amasa Delano—Jack of the Beach, as they called me when a lad—I, Amasa . . . to be murdered here at the ends of the earth, on board a haunted pirate ship by a horrible Spaniard? Too nonsensical to think of! Who would murder Amasa Delano? His conscience is clean. There is someone above. Fie, Fie, Jack of the Beach! you are a child indeed; a child of the second childhood, old boy; you are beginning to dote and drule, I'm afraid." [P. 92]

When a text has a character warning himself that he is "beginning to dote and drule," the critical reader might legitimately read the ironic distance signified as insufficiently measured by notions of "naiveté," or "undistrustful good nature." And when the text, a few sentences later, puts in Delano's head the words: "Ha! glancing towards the boat; there *Rover;* good dog; a white bone in her mouth. A pretty big bone though, seems to me," one can easily read an association between Delano's image of the surf seen as a "bone" in the mouth of his boat and the image of the skeleton affixed to the prow of the *San Dominick*—a bone on which this ideology will have to choke. Captain Delano of the *Bachelor's Delight* seems to have a "good nature" much like that of those other Melvillean bachelors:

> For these men of wealth, pain and trouble simply do not exist: the thing called pain, the bugbear called trouble—those two legends seemed preposterous to their bachelor imaginations. How could men of liberal sense, ripe scholarship in the world, and capacious philosophical and convivial understandings—how could they suffer themselves to be imposed upon by such monkish fables? Pain! Trouble! As well talk of Catholic miracles. No such thing.—Pass the sherry, sir.—Pooh, pooh! Can't be![36]

If ideology is a kind of preconscious grid that prestructures all experience (and any idea) in a form tending to validate those held within the ideology, a certain Yankee bourgeois ideology confirms precisely this social self-perception as "men of liberal sense." It has been something of an ironic fate for "Benito Cereno" that its simultaneous internalization of and distantiation from this ideology have allowed critical readings to mistake for their object, rather than ideology, the "problem of the blacks" or "the problem of evil"—thereby "drowning criticism in compassion" (p. 69) and presenting this text as safe for all "men of liberal sense." Take the following excerpt from a criticism that sincerely tries to account for the text's ironic distance from Delano's attitude toward the blacks:

> The fascinating enigma of *Benito Cereno* revolves around the question of what Melville intended his blacks to be. . . .
>
> *Benito Cereno* is neither an abolitionist tract nor a condemnation of the Negro race. Evil and ferocity are not confined to the blacks; heroism and virtue are not the exclusive trait of the whites. Both blacks and whites are part of the humanity whose dark side Melville will not deny. Babo is part man, part beast. . . . But the white man, who ironically espouses a religion of . . . brotherhood, is also a beast. Who can say where the blame rests for the carnage unleashed aboard the flaming coffin? The untamed and daemonic forces rampant on the *San Dominick* characterize . . . all of mankind.[37]

By taking as its starting point that Melville's text is about "his" blacks rather than "about" ideology because "of" ideology, this reading follows the road of good intentions into a certain humanist ideological cul-de-sac. We can almost see Delano and his confreres of "liberal sense and ripe scholarship" nodding with approval at hearing that everyone has a dark side and a light side, is half-man and half-beast, and we can hear the whispered "Not me!" in response to the comforting rhetorical query: "Who can say where the blame rests?" For "men of liberal sense" the "carnage" and "daemonic forces" that provide the conditions of their own social possibility remain unspoken problems in a moralizing discourse about the problem of the blacks or the problem of evil.

But "Benito Cereno" tenaciously refuses to let Delano's ideological "set" off its ironic hook. In fact, the text explicitly images Delano's ideological sense of his own innocence as not just naiveté (not just a mistake based on that innocence!), but as the condition of a deliberate, unnecessary, and massively lethal violence. Such a sharp assertion can be ratified in that textual moment when, after realizing that he has been fooled to the last minute and beyond by the blacks' manipulation of his ideology, Delano orders his men to attack the *San Dominick* and recover control from the rebellious slaves:

> Upon inquiring of Don Benito what firearms they had on board the *San Dominick,* Captain Delano was answered that they had none that could be used; because, in the earlier stages of the mutiny, a cabin-passenger, since dead, had secretly put out of order the locks of what few muskets there were. But with all his remaining strength, Don Benito entreated the American not to give chase, either with ship or boat; for . . . in the case of a present assault, nothing but a total massacre of the whites could be looked for. But, regarding this warning as coming from one whose spirit had been crushed by misery, the American did not give up his design.
>
> The boats were got ready and armed. . . .
>
> The officers . . . for reasons connected with their interests and those of the voyage, and a duty owing to the owners, strongly objected against their commander's going. Weighing their remonstrances a moment, Captain Delano felt bound to remain; appointing his chief mate—an athletic and resolute man, who had been a privateer's-man—to head the party. The more to encourage the sailors, they were told, that the Spanish captain considered this ship good as lost; that she and her cargo, including some gold and silver, were worth more than a thousand doubloons. Take her, and no small part should be theirs. The sailors replied with a shout. [P. 120][38]

This passage gives the reader some definite textual characterizations of Delano. 1) Delano knows that the blacks are effectively unarmed *and* that they are unaware of this disadvantage, since the firearms have been "secretly put out of order." (Indeed, heroism is "not the exclusive trait of the whites.") 2) Delano is unconcerned about the possible mass slaughter of blacks *and* whites, and insists on pursuing his scheme forcibly to restore the "real" in its proper image of order, despite the impassioned plea ("with all his remaining strength") of Cereno, who has the only semblance of "real" interest in recapturing the *San Dominick.* Delano, because of his class-political position as the representative of the interests of the officers and owners as a whole,[39] piously refrains from going, and sends to lead the charge his chief mate, an ex-pirate (the kind of subordinate whom men like Delano often keep around to do their "police" work). 3) Again, the simple textual movement of a phrase set off by commas—"they were told"—establishes subtly but definitely that Delano lies to his own men, provoking their greed in order to encourage their participation in a deadly expedition in which they have absolutely no real interest. "They were told," "the more to encourage them," that the *San*

Dominick contained gold and silver, but the text gives two inventories of the ship's cargo, and in neither is there any mention of this inspirational gold and silver.[40] The communicative intention here, what the text "lets the reader know," is not that there *was* gold, but that Delano *said* there was and why he said it. The text here again communicates that Delano's discourse is the "subject" of its own, that his ideology—his politically and unconsciously overdetermined "lived relation to the real," as enacted in word and deed—is the "object" taken as its "problem."

Delano's ideology reveals at the core of its innocence and "whiteness," a skeletal infrastructure that is death and violence. Not only does the *San Dominick* have "death for the figurehead, in a human skeleton; chalky comment on the chalked words below, *'Follow Your Leader'*" (p. 119), it also has death for its savior—death in the form of a live whiteness sent by Delano through the agency of his first mate. If the reader but recall the text's rendering of Delano's early spontaneous perception of the blacks:

> There's naked nature, now; pure tenderness and love, thought Captain Delano, well pleased.
> This incident prompted him to remark the other negresses more particularly than before. He was gratified with their manners: like most uncivilized women, they seemed at once tender of heart and tough of constitution; equally ready to die for their infants or fight for them. Unsophisticated as leopardesses; loving as doves. Ah! thought Captain Delano. . . . [P. 87]

—if the reader but *read* Delano's pleasure and gratification at this "primitive" tenderness and strength, under the text's rendering of the following scene of attack on the *San Dominick,* then "Benito Cereno" will register all its scathing ironic effect, irrevocably displaying the cruelty and hypocrisy of Delano's "lived relation to the real." This scene, at once lyrical and cynical in its evocation of the desperate but futile struggle of the blacks, and the text in which it is set, can be read as achieving at least one aspect of authorial intention with unanticipated force, presenting "another world, and yet one to which we feel the tie":

> With creaking masts, she came heavily round to the wind; the prow slowly swinging into view of the boats, its skeleton gleaming in the horizontal moonlight, and casting a gigantic ribbed shadow

upon the water. One extended arm of the ghost seemed beckoning the whites to avenge it.

"Follow your leader!" cried the mate; and, one on each bow, the boats boarded. Sealing spears and cutlasses crossed hatchets and handspikes. Huddled among the longboat amidships, the negresses raised a wailing chant, whose chorus was the clash of the steel.

For a time, the attack wavered; the negroes wedging themselves to beat it back; the half-repelled sailors, as yet unable to gain a footing, fighting as troopers in the saddle, one leg sideways flung over the bulwarks, and one without, plying their cutlasses like carters' whips. But in vain. They were almost overborne, when, rallying themselves into a squad as one man, with a huzza, they sprang inboard, where, entangled, they involuntarily separated again. For a few breaths' space, there was a vague, muffled, inner sound, as of submerged sword-fish rushing hither and thither through shoals of black-fish. Soon, in a reunited band, and joined by the Spanish seamen, the whites came to the surface, irresistibly driving the negroes toward the stern. But a barricade of casks and sacks, from side to side, had been thrown up by the mainmast. Here the negroes faced about, and though scorning peace or truce, yet fain would have had respite. But, without pause, overleaping the barrier, the unflagging sailors again closed. Exhausted, the blacks now fought in despair. Their red tongues lolled, wolf-like, from their black mouths. But the pale sailors' teeth were set; not a word was spoken; and, in five minutes more, the ship was won. [P. 122][41]

This rendering of the personal courage of black men and women is a remarkable achievement in American literature for any year, let alone 1855. Even the white sailors' courage stands as an implicit indictment of Delano, the absent author of this senseless slaughter, who can rely on others to enforce his peculiar sense of justice. And the simple textual movement of "as troopers in the saddle" and "like carters' whips" marks this text as, indeed, no mere "abolitionist tract" but a resonant gloss on the history of a civilization. In a characteristic Melvillean trope, the scene closes where the literary ends, in a space where words cannot be spoken.[42]

Certainly, Melville's text gives us the blacks as uncompromising in their use of force, deception (but not self-deception), and courage to resist enslavement; then it gives us Delano (not "the whites")[43] as ruthless in his use of violence, deception, and the manipulation of the greed and courage of others to annihilate any challenge to his self-deceiving "reality" of power, authority, and superiority. And if one is to choose how to "read" this carefully specified situation (as the reader must, and does), it is of no help for criticism to translate the text into a metaphysics of light versus dark, or man versus beast, terms whose only possible function is to make a choice seem impossible by offering ambivalence as the only possible choice.

Delano's violent repression of the blacks, against Cereno's own entreaties, seeks to reconstruct that comforting order of things in which other men take their proper relation to him, a relation like that of "Newfoundland dogs." Delano wants to believe—wants really to *see*—this order, not as "constructed" by his own egotistical and violent practices, but as "justified" by his own essential innocence. Cereno's deposition, forming a separate part of the narrative, serves only to underscore Delano's bad faith. Repeating the phrase "the noble Captain Amasa Delano" evokes a ritual courtroom litany that the critical reader should take less as a sincere expression of Cereno's respect than an ironic designation of the Yankee trader as the kind of "gentleman" whom the decadent Spanish aristocracy recognizes as one of its own. And Delano's assertion of a moral distance from the actions of his subordinates, in stopping "with his own hand" sailors' attempts to kill "shackled negroes," must be understood in relation to his responsibility for instigating the slaughter. For Delano, the American, the sense of his own innocence and good will serves as a precondition for the forcible maintenance of political and social relations that support his privilege. In the ideological discourse of a man like Delano, of the "civilization" that produces such men, the use of armed force must never be understood for what it is (the social equivalent of the oppressive feudal violence of aristocrats and slaveowners), but as a mistake resulting from an excess of goodness, a mistake to be abolished from memory and history as quickly as possible.

But Cereno, the European, knows better. And while Delano restores the order of this world, with his own "good nature" as its imaginary linchpin, Cereno finds himself unable to continue in self-deception, unable to ignore that death-dealing which is the real linchpin of the social order, unable, it seems, even to exist as he was before. In the last section of the narrative, we find a final, telling exchange between Cereno and Delano. Both now possess full knowledge of the events aboard the *San Dominick,* but only one has been dislodged from his ideological lived relation to a specular, self-justifying "real." The American's desperate, insane plea for the saving power of his own innocence and closeness to Providence now rings especially hollow against the Spaniard's polite but definite charge of responsibility, and against Cereno's own profound self-transformation, even self-dissolution:

> ". . . you have saved my life, Don Benito, more than I yours; saved it, too, against my knowledge and will."
>
> "Nay, my friend," rejoined the Spaniard, courteous even to the point of religion, "God charmed your life, but you saved mine. To think of some of the things you did—those smilings and chattings, rash pointings and gesturings. For less than these, they slew my mate, Raneds; but you had the Prince of Heaven's safe conduct."
>
> "Yes, all is owing to Providence, I know: but the temper of my mind that morning was more than commonly pleasant, while the sight of so much suffering, more apparent than real, added to my good-nature, compassion, and charity, happily interweaving the three. Had it been otherwise, doubtless, as you hint, some of my interferences might have ended unhappily enough. . . . Only at the end, did my suspicions get the better of me, and you know how wide of the mark they then proved."
>
> "Wide, indeed," said Don Benito sadly; "you were with me all day; stood with me, looked at me, ate with me, drank with me; and yet, your last act was to clutch for a monster, not only an innocent man, but the most pitiable of all men. To such degree may malign machinations and deceptions impose. So far may even the best men err in judging the conduct of one with the recesses of whose condition he is not acquainted." [Pp. 138–39][44]

Cereno, "courteous even to the point of religion," speaks in a discourse informed by the ironic nuance of the text. He speaks of Delano's protection by "the Prince of Heaven": the reader might easily infer that the text means Christ, but is not Christ a King?[45] And what was Delano's "last act"? When he lashed out at Cereno, was that the *last* time he lashed out at "the most pitiable of all men," the kind of man "with the recesses of whose condition he is not acquainted"? Does the text here mean Christ or Satan, Aristocrat or Slave? The phrases speak for themselves, but the reader must decide what they say. The textual ambiguity cannot be resolved by peering into the blinding light of the words themselves, but only in that shadow cast upon them by an unspoken relation to an ideology.

So Cereno, in the shadow of ideology, wastes away and dies, knowing without illusion what he was and is, but unable to communicate why "the negro" still haunts him, and why it might come back to haunt the Yankee himself. "Slowly and unconsciously gathering his mantle about him, as if it were a pall," Cereno falls deadly silent: "There was no more conversation that day" (p. 139). Again, the text marks a space where words must end. Cereno remains unable to speak of the empty inscriptions of his rank and command—the ceremonial dress, sword, and scabbard he was forced to don for Delano; he refuses to confirm Babo's identity as the accused.[46] Having been made to occupy the position of the slave—having been forced to choke on the ideology of the master—Cereno, like Babo, stands mute, knowing the futility of speech in the face of an infinite, closed ideological discourse whose only pronouncement can be, whose every pronouncement is, death. In death, Babo's decapitated gaze forms a circuit of silent communication with Cereno and Aranda, a circuit of complicity in which each acknowledges the shared burden of death, violence, and oppression—a circuit from which Amasa Delano is excluded not, as he might like to believe, because he is any better or any more innocent than they are, but only because he thinks that he is. And in the final scene of the text, the characters fall on either side of a divide, not of race or even of slavery, but of ideology—of the ability to continue living within social relations whose precondition is the discourse of self-deception:

> Some months after, dragged to the gibbet at the tail of a mule, the black met his voiceless end. The body was burned to ashes; but for many days, the head, that hive of subtlety, fixed on a pole in the Plaza, met, unabashed, the gaze of the whites; and across the Plaza looked towards St. Bartholomew's church, in whose vaults slept then, as now, the recovered bones of Aranda; and across the Rimac bridge looked towards the monastery, on Mount Agonia without; where, three months after being dismissed by the court, Benito Cereno, borne on the bier, did, indeed, follow his leader. [P. 140]

The text here is not quite "frozen into silence," but has written its way into that final, "voiceless" space where words no longer rule. This laden silence is a characteristic Melvillean ending, invoking a sense of futile defiance in the face of an ideological, "literary" discursivity that often, like the following, pronounces the text's decapitation in order to immortalize, universalize, and enshrine it as an object of specular fascination for a dominant "lived relation to the real":

> The primary theme of "Benito Cereno," determined by Melville's emphasis, is Delano's struggle to comprehend the action. . . . At the end two conclusions are made about the meaning of the facts: first, that reality is a mystery and hard to read, and second, that evil is real and must be reckoned with. To which should perhaps be added, there are some evils that are cureless and some

> mysteries insoluble to man. . . . The mystery of "Benito Cereno" is a mystery of evil, contrived by an evil will [Babo's]. . . .
>
> Delano has one vital disability. . . . He does not understand "of what humanity is capable." Beyond this, the problem is real. It is the creation of a complex and malignant mind [Babo's], a "hive of subtlety," which has deliberately contrived its confusions.[47]

Such a reading ignores all the incisive ideological effect of a text that evokes with ironic precision the first triumphal period of bourgeois revolutionary ideals, even while written as the bankruptcy of those ideals is being seriously challenged by popular struggles. Such a reading can only dilute the power of a text that, written on the eve of a civil war over slavery, speaks beyond even the issue of slavery to racial oppression as a constant shadow within general questions of political and social relations—questions to which even the "Northerner" is blind. Such a reading dispels all the formal tension of a work that strains implicitly to articulate a radical, devastating critique of an ideology that it is constrained explicitly to enter. Indeed, such a reading, with its "reality is a mystery" and "evil is real," marks "Benito Cereno's" passage into the court of a "literary" ideological apparatus—its self-anticipated fate, for which it prepared its own ambiguous silences.

But our historical and ideological conjecture allows us to restore the strong voice of this text's irony. We can encourage it to give, not cringing witness against itself, but compelling testimony, that its prosecutors, who for the moment must listen, do not want to hear—namely, that the "mystery" of violence and social oppression can only be disclosed through analysis and dissolution of that even more complex and malignant "hive of subtlety" which deliberately contrives its own confusions: the ideology of men like the "good American," Amasa Delano.

Notes

1. Vernon Louis Parrington, *Main Currents in American Thought*, vol. 2, *The Romantic Revolution in America* (New York: Harcourt, 1930), pp. 258–67.

2. George Washington Peck, in *Melville: The Critical Heritage*, ed. Watson G. Branch (Boston: Routledge & Kegan Paul, 1974), pp. 316–17, 321.

3. Between 1863 and 1887, for example, an average of twenty-three copies of *Moby Dick* were sold in the United States each year; after the first Melville "revival" (centering on *Moby Dick*), between 1921 and 1947, the book sold more than one million copies. See H. Hetherington, *Melville's Reviewers: British and American, 1846–1971* (Chapel Hill:

University of North Carolina Press, 1961), p. 221. George Thomas Tanselle notes that, of the fifty-six editions of *Moby Dick,* half have been published during the last twenty-five years, and all but six after 1920, with many more copies of the book sold each year now than the total sold in the nineteenth century. See Tanselle's *A Checklist of Editions of Moby Dick, 1851–1976* (Evanston, Ill.: Northwestern University Press, 1976).

4. According to F. O. Matthiessen, in *From the Heart of Europe* (New York: Oxford University Press, 1948), p. 45, *Moby Dick* was still catalogued under "Cetology" in 1930.

5. I make no claim to account for any representative "cross section" of the voluminous Melville criticism. By "paradigmatic" readings, I mean those that have set the terms for critical debate over a long period, and have been the most widely anthologized. In Richard V. Chase, ed., *Melville: A Collection of Critical Essays* (Englewood Cliffs, N.J.: Prentice-Hall, 1962), for example, we find articles by Matthiessen, Arvin, Fogle, and Chase himself. These readings have formed a kind of unavoidable threshold for Melville readers.

6. F. O. Matthiessen, *American Renaissance* (New York: Oxford University Press, 1941), p. 508.

7. Leslie Fiedler, *Love and Death in the American Novel* (Cleveland, Ohio: Meridian Books, 1962), pp. 400–401. See also Chase's *Herman Melville: A Critical Study* (New York: Macmillan, 1949), p. 157, where he asserts that Captain Delano is "a benevolent and courageous man."

8. See Warner Berthoff, *The Example of Melville* (Princeton, N.J.: Princeton University Press, 1962), p. 153. See also Lawrance Thompson, *Melville's Quarrel with God* (Princeton, N.J.: Princeton University Press, 1952), passim. Interesting, too, is the chapter on "Benito Cereno" in William B. Dillingham, *Melville's Short Fiction, 1853–1856* (Athens, Ga: University of Georgia Press, 1977), pp. 227–70. Note also the argument Fiedler implies above: that Melville's attitudes toward slavery are analogous to Delano's because his regional origins are analogous to Delano's.

9. H. Bruce Franklin's work, asserting that Melville was a "consciously proletarian writer," provides the best example of this implicit justification. See H. Bruce Franklin, "Herman Melville: Artist of the Worker's World," in Norman Rudich, ed., *Weapons of Criticism: Marxism in America and the Literary Tradition* (Palo Alto, Calif.: Ramparts Press, 1976), pp. 287–310; "On the Teaching of Literature in the Highest Academies of the Empire," in Louis Kampf and Paul Lauter, eds., *The Politics of Literature: Dissenting Essays in the Teaching of English* (New York: Pantheon Books, 1972), pp. 101–29; and H. Bruce Franklin, *The Victim as Criminal and Artist* (New York: Oxford University Press, 1978), pp. 31–72. See also Marvin Fisher's strong treatment in *Going Under: Melville's Short Fiction and the American 1850s* (Baton Rouge, La: Louisiana State University Press, 1977). Many readings of "Benito Cereno" have strayed outside the dominant critical paradigms, and are as a result much less widely known; examples include: E. F. Carlisle, "Captain Amasa Delano: Melville's American Fool," *Criticism* 7, no. 4 (Fall 1965): 349–62; Joseph Schiffman, "Critical Problems in 'Benito Cereno'," *Modern Language Quarterly* 11, no. 3 (September 1950): 317–24; Jean Fagin Yellin, "Black Masks: Melville's 'Benito Cereno'," *American Quarterly* 22, no. 3 (Fall 1970): 678–89; Jack Matlack, "Attica and Melville's 'Benito Cereno'," *American Transcendental Quarterly,* No. 26 (supplement, Spring 1975): 18–23; Glenn C. Altschuler, "Whose Foot on Whose Throat? A Re-examination of 'Benito Cereno'," *College Language Association Journal* 18, no. 3 (March 1975): 383–92. Theoretical differences notwithstanding, I find all these readings cogent, and support their ideological effect; they also highlight in various ways much of what I foreground from Melville's text.

10. See Terence Eagleton, *Criticism and Ideology* (London: New Left Books, 1976),

especially chapters two and three on the literary text as putting ideology into production.

11. Newton Arvin, *Herman Melville* (New York: Sloane, 1950), pp. 239–40.

12. Louis Althusser, *For Marx* (New York: Vintage Books, 1970), pp. 232–33.

13. Louis Althusser, *Lenin and Philosophy and Other Essays* (New York: Monthly Review Press, 1971), pp. 222–23.

14. Amasa Delano, *Narrative of Voyages and Travels in the Northern and Southern Hemispheres comprising Three Voyages Around the World together with a Voyage of Survey and Discovery in the Pacific and Oriental Islands* (Boston: E. G. House, 1817), privately printed for the author. This edition bears the seal of William S. Shaw, District Clerk of Massachusetts, probably related to Lemuel Shaw, the Chief Justice of Massachusetts and Melville's father-in-law.

15. See Eagleton, *Criticism and Ideology*, pp. 66–90. I emphasize that Melville's ideological intentions enter this process *as* raw materials, subject to specific transformations.

16. Under the pressures of Stalinism, Marxism has not rigorously worked out the primary thrust of Marx and Engels's few writings on literature and art: the insistence that there is *no* necessary congruence between the ideological opinions or intentions of an author and the ideological significance or effect of a text. See Lee Baxandall and Stefan Morawski, eds., *Marx and Engels on Literature and Art* (New York: International General, 1974), especially pp. 119–31 on "tendency literature."

17. Althusser, *Lenin and Philosophy*, p. 223.

18. This point implies the need for long quotations from the text in the analysis. Criticism cannot act as if the long, complicated sentences and paragraphs that constitute the *ériture* of the text do not exist. If criticism is to take the first "naive" reading as its object, it must reproduce, as its internal evidence, the experience of that first reading. "Benito Cereno" can test the patience of both reader and critic in this regard, but even some of the better criticism has suffered, I believe, from attempting to analyze the story based on selected *phrases* and sentences.

19. Berthoff, *The Example of Melville*, p. 153.

20. Jay Leyda, ed., *The Portable Melville* (New York: Penguin Books, 1976), p. 430.

21. Fisher, in *Going Under*, gives a strong account of Melville as a writer who "went underground."

22. American New Criticism might, however, be more interesting and contradictory in this regard than its left critics generally concede.

23. Arvin, *Herman Melville*, p. 239.

24. Preface to "Billy Budd," in Leyda, *The Portable Melville*, p. 637.

25. Ibid.

26. Herman Melville, "Benito Cereno," in *The Piazza Tales* (New York: Hendricks House, Farrar Strauss, 1948), p. 105. This text is an exact copy of the first edition of *The Piazza Tales*, which Melville himself prepared from the original *Putnam's Monthly Magazine* version of the story, making some changes. Further citations are referenced in my essay by page numbers from the Hendricks House edition, with footnotes clarifying any of Melville's changes from the *Putnam* version.

27. The *Amistad* rebellion (in which Spaniards and Americans fought over captured slaves) had a progressive denouement, with the Supreme Court freeing the insurgent slaves rather than sending them back. See J. Q. Adams, *Arguments of John Quincy Adams before the Supreme Court of the United States, in the case of the U. S. Appellants vs. Cinque, and other Africans, Captured in the Schooner Amistad* (New York, 1841); but this trend was reversed near the time Melville wrote "Benito Cereno," with the Supreme Court deci-

sion to return fugitive slaves Thomas Sims and Anthony Burns. The *Creole* incident, the Nat Turner rebellion, and the Toussaint L'Ouverture uprising have all been mentioned as possible historical raw materials for Melville's text. See Altschuler, "Whose Foot on Whose Throat?", pp. 388–89, and Fisher, *Going Under,* pp. 109, 116.

28. If this seems a convoluted reading of the sentence, the syntax, I believe, allows it. The aptness of such a reading would depend on how one construes the point the sentence is trying to make, and one's spontaneous construal of that point is exactly what the critical reader cannot take for granted. In general, moreover, *any* reading of a sentence in this text is somewhat convoluted. Rather than seeing this problem in terms of an infinitely repeating hermeneutic circularity, I suggest seeing these sentences as determinately undecidable—undecidable, that is, except on taking up one of the finite number of determinate positions that would decide a meaning.

29. The reader does not learn of the old man's death until p. 135.

30. A *loose* reference to the Althusserian concept of "symptomatic reading." See *For Marx,* pp. 69–70, and Althusser and Etienne Balibar, *Reading Capital* (London: New Left Books, 1975), pp. 32–33.

31. Althusser, *For Marx,* p. 234.

32. This passage also explicitly alludes to the need for such "police officers" on an "emigrant ship"; in his *Narrative,* the real Captain Delano worries about a possible mutiny on his own ship when he comes upon the Spanish slaver.

33. Strictly speaking, one should say that the text "knows" nothing, but that, in giving a "reading," criticism must construct either a "text" that operates *as if* it knows what is going on here, or one that operates as if it does not, and that the latter construction would require a critical labor at least as peculiar, controverted, and heavily ideologically determined as the former.

34. See Eagleton, *Criticism and Ideology,* chap. 3.

35. Matthiessen, *American Renaissance,* p. 508.

36. Herman Melville, "The Paradise of Bachelors and The Tartarus of Maids," in Warner Berthoff, ed., *The Great Short Works of Herman Melville* (New York: Harper, 1969), p. 209.

37. Edward S. Grejda, *The Common Content of Men: Racial Equality in the Writings of Herman Melville* (Port Washington, N.Y.: Kennikat Press, 1974), pp. 136, 147. For a view which finds Melville regressively reproducing racist stereotypes, see Sidney Kaplan, "Herman Melville and the American National Sin," in Seymour L. Gross and John Edward Hardy, eds., *Images of the Negro in American Literature* (Chicago: University of Chicago Press, 1966), pp. 135–62; this article first appeared in *Journal of Negro History* 41 (1956): 311–38; 42 (1957): 11–37. Its inclusion, along with Fiedler's section on "Benito Cereno," in a 1972 anthology underscores my point about the tenacity of "paradigmatic readings" within the ideological practice of literary criticism.

38. The original text in *Putnam's Monthly Magazine of American Literature, Science, and Arts,* July-December 1855, p. 636, reads: "a privateer's man, and, as his enemies whispered, a pirate."

39. This straight Marxist gloss on Melville's phrase beginning "for reasons connected with their interests," suggests some of the problems in attempting to have the "real" Herman Melville ratify a textual reading. Whether the "real" Herman Melville would have made or would have agreed with such a restatement himself (knowing all its theoretical and political implications) is, strictly speaking, irrelevant; it remains a fair reading of the sentence in the text, as "close" as any that could be given.

40. Cereno gives the first inventory on p. 65: "a general cargo, hardware, Paraguay

tea and the like—and . . . that parcel of negroes"; the *Putnam* text (p. 358) omits "hardware." Melville's deliberate additions to the cargo inventories for the *Piazza Tales* edition can give an "intentional" *defense* (not positive support) for reading the omission of the gold and silver (which Delano's 1818 *Narrative* does mention explicitly) as a "significant absence." Characteristically, too, the text never tells us that the sailors *got* any gold or silver, only that Delano, in typically evasive fashion, *promised* them "no small amount"; since "nothing" is indeed "no small amount," Delano's discourse, even here, constructs itself so as to avoid any kind of positive, unambiguous self-definition for which he could be held accountable.

41. The *Putnam* text (p. 637) includes a comma after "swinging."

42. I find that this recurrent Melvillean gesture of ending in silence symptomatizes a suspicion, even a refusal, of the mode in which further literary discourse would recuperate the text. It is almost as if Melville were signaling in the text: "This is where *literary* analysis must stop," a signal displaced just enough so that literary analysis can take its very silence as a clue for endless commentary.

43. The white American sailors, as indicated, are deceived into jeopardizing their lives for no interest of their own; two of the white Spanish sailors are deliberately killed in the boarding on the suspicion that they "favored the cause of the negroes" (p. 136).

44. The *Putnam* text reads "clutch for a villain." This again indicates the problem with searching for authorial ratification for a reading. Although we can probably never know Melville's reason for this seemingly minute revision, his deliberate replacement of "villain" with "monster" gives a connotation and an objective indeterminacy of meaning that supports the Cereno/Babo ambivalence I suggest we can read in the word.

45. A well-known (certainly to Melville) literary example of the Prince-King relationship alluded to here is in Beelzebub's speech to Satan in *Paradise Lost* 1:128–32: "O Prince, O Chief of many thronèd Powers / That led the embattled Seraphim to war / Under thy conduct, and, in dreadful deeds / Fearless, endangered Heaven's perpetual King, / And put to proof his high supremacy."

46. "Before the tribunal he refused. When pressed by the judges he fainted. On the testimony of the sailors alone rested the legal identity of Babo" (p. 140).

47. Richard Harter Fogle, *Melville's Shorter Tales* (Norman, Okla.: University of Oklahoma Press, 1960), pp. 120–21, 124–25.

Poetry and Kingship: Shakespeare's *A Midsummer Night's Dream*

Leo Paul S. de Alvarez

University of Dallas

THE rule of Theseus is challenged at the beginning of the play by the old law of Athens.[1] Yet at the end of the play Theseus is able to set aside the old law, permitting the young couples to marry according to their "natural taste." What has occurred in the intervening time that allows Theseus to say to Egeus, "I will overbear your will"? Are the dreamlike episodes in the woods the necessary preparation for the happy establishment of Theseus's rule? Despite his rejection of the reports of the lovers as "antic fables" and "fairy toys" or, as Hippolyta says, "fancy's images," it is yet his household that is blessed by the fairies. Theseus's much quoted lines on the "lunatic, the lover, and the poet" are taken as showing him to have no true appreciation of poetry, but the fairies are the bringers of grace to his household, and the rule of a king ought always to begin with the proper ordering of his household.

The events in the woods take place in a world that is like a dream. And yet these events are of such a character that those who experience them cannot remember if they were dreams or not. We ourselves do not know, for what happens in the woods to the lovers and the craftsmen is not presented to us as dreams. Puck speaks of the events of the entire play as visions, which are "No more yielding than a dream," but the play requires us, like Hermia, to have a double vision. We have the double worlds of woods and city, of the play within the play, and then the dream of fairies in the woods suddenly becomes the dream that is the poem or play.[2]

No other work of Shakespeare's so deliberately plays upon the experience of dramatic or mimetic action.[3] The arguments between Bottom and Peter Quince over how best to represent the moon and moonshine, the comments of the ducal audience as they watch Pyramus and Thisbe, and especially the interweaving of fairies in the woods and the play within the play, make of *A Midsummer Night's Dream* the play in which we seem to be expected to reflect upon the power of similitudes or images upon our souls.

The power of images and the founding of a city appear then to be the two themes of the *Dream.* It is the only play of Shakespeare's in which the founder of a great city is a character. The great founders of classical antiquity are usually said to be Lycurgus, Theseus, Romulus, and perhaps Solon and Numa. Of this list, Shakespeare treats only of Theseus, but Theseus and his deeds are not the substance of the play. Instead we are told of the misapprehensions and quarrels of runaway lovers, of Athenian artisans who are rehearsing a play, and of the encounter of these two groups with the world of the fairies. Why should it be Theseus, of all the political founders, whom Shakespeare chooses to be the recipient of fairy blessing and not, say, Lycurgus or Romulus or some ancient British king?

The marriage of Theseus and Hippolyta frames the action of the *Dream.* Theseus's world is the waking world, in which the fairy visions are to be permitted to exist only as faintly remembered things. Even Bottom knows that "Man is but an ass, if he go about to expound this dream." And yet the vision in the woods profoundly affects the city, for among other things it makes Demetrius a better man.

The dream of Midsummer Night is then the experience of the fairy world in the woods. It is also, and perhaps above all, called Bottom's Dream. And Puck says that it is the play itself. It is a dream that is to be dreamt on Midsummer Night—or so I interpret the title—to be dreamt, that is to say, on the shortest night of the year. Whether the action of the drama takes place on Midsummer Night is, it seems to me, of little importance. The argument has been made that the action takes place on May Day's eve,[4] but the references are ambiguous;[5] what is said is that the place in the woods to which the lovers repair and where they are found sleeping is where the rites of May are usually celebrated. However, time and season are so confused in the play, as we shall see, that it seems characteristic that the time and season of its events should also be confused.[6] We are left, therefore, even more curious as to why the title should refer to Midsummer Night. Nothing in the action of the play itself directly suggests why it should. Of course to title it *A May Day's Eve's Dream* would seem to be awkward. But is there anything in the traditions of Midsummer Night that might help us? We know that the festivities of that night are a celebration of the sun, and the main custom observed is the burning of fires on hilltops throughout the night as the dawn is awaited. One possible link is that it is a night when maidens might find their true love in their dreams. However, the general conclusion on this subject is that Shakespeare is not governed by whatever traditions existed, but is rather freely using them to his own purposes, much as he does with the traditions regarding the fairies.[7] In other words, the significance of Shakespeare's Midsummer Night is not to be found by consulting books of English or German folklore, but only by understanding the play itself. We are to be given the dream that is to be dreamt on the shortest night of the year. What would such a dream be, and why should such a dream be the one the poet should choose to present? We are also led to conclude that a Midsummer Night's dream is one of especial significance for the ruler or founder of a city.

I

The wedding plans of Theseus and Hippolyta open the play. We remind ourselves first of the stories about these two. Theseus is the great Greek hero, second only to Heracles. He unified the villages of Attica into one city, "ordaining," says Plutarch, "a common feast and sacrifice, which he called Panathenaea, or the sacrifice of all the united Athenians." Plutarch also tells us that he belonged to an age that "produced a sort of men, in force of hand, and swiftness of foot, and strength of body, excelling the ordinary." That strength of body, however, was used by such men "to no good or profitable purpose for mankind." The difference between Heracles and Theseus has been said to be that Heracles overcame inhuman or superhuman foes; Theseus usually fought against human enemies, the brutal men who used their natural strength of body and mind for their own wicked purposes. Theseus overcame all those who would do harm; he thus made civilization possible by destroying the unjust. He always sought to be popular, invited strangers into the city, and made of Athens, according to Plutarch, not only "a commonwealth, in a manner, for all nations," but also a city that was, "as it were, reduced to an exact equality, the nobles excelling the rest in honour, the husbandmen in profit, and the artificers in number."[8] Theseus was a pacifying, civilizing, and popularizing force.

Hippolyta is the Queen of the Amazons. The Amazons waged two wars against Theseus. In the first, Theseus and Heracles led an expedition to obtain Hippolyta's girdle as one of the labors of Heracles. In the second, the Amazons invaded Attica, took the Areopagus, and besieged but could not capture the Acropolis. There was a great battle; the Amazons were defeated and agreed to withdraw. The event was commemorated by sculptures on the Parthenon, on the metopes of the West end and on the shield of the image of the goddess within the temple. It is not clear from the stories whether Hippolyta or Antiope fought with or against Theseus in the siege of the Acropolis. I am certainly tempted to adopt the version that says Hippolyta was wounded and captured in the attack and to infer, therefore, that the play begins immediately after the Amazons' defeat and withdrawal from Attica. When Theseus promises Hippolyta that although he has begun by injuring her he will "wed her in another key," I believe we are meant to be reminded of the recent Amazon invasion.

That invasion was thought to have been the first invasion of Athens by barbarians from the East, and therefore a foreshadowing of the Persian invasion. But there is a deeper significance. In the Parthenon sculptures, the parallel to the Amazonomachy of the West end of the temple is the Gigantomachy of the East end.[9] As the heavenly gods of Olympus had to put down the giants of the earth, so too did the Athenians have to war against barbarian women from the East. Disorder and barbarism appear in various particular forms, but the enemy is the same. The wedding festivities that open the play would, then, have followed upon a difficult war in which the powerful and eternal enemies of Athens have once again been met.

The wedding is to coincide with the change of the moon,

which is to come in four days. Meanwhile, the Athenians are to give themselves overto merriment. If a hard war has recently been concluded, there may be great need for merriment. To be sure, no such thoughts are directly evoked, but what of the reference to Hippolyta's injuries? How did she receive them and how recently?

II

The wedding festivities are threatened by the complaint of Egeus, an old Athenian citizen, who asks that his daughter, Hermia, either be forced to obey him or else be put to death. The name Egeus has an odd resonance. We remember that Theseus's father was named Aegeus, and that there had always been a dark doubt as to the manner of Aegeus's death. Plutarch says plainly, "Theseus, in his forgetfulness and neglect of the command concerning the flag, can scarcely, methinks, by any excuses, or before the most indulgent judges, avoid the imputation of parricide."[10] Only after the parricide, however, does "the great and wonderful design" of Athenian unity come into effect. Does Theseus see the ancient order rising to threaten him?

We have, in a way, been prepared for this confrontation with the old by Theseus's first speech, which is the first speech of the entire play. Theseus complains of the slowness of the waning of the old moon, and likens it to an old dowager who prevents a young man from realizing his desires because of her power over his money. Youthful desire is stayed by the economic power of the old. But if we think on it, the economic power of the old can only exist if it is upheld by the power of the law. It is the law, as we soon see, that is the critical issue.

The moon and its changes are of considerable importance in this play, and we have to pay attention to the moon at the very beginning.[11] We first hear that the changes of the moon are used to mark the changes in human affairs. A certain event will happen at a certain phase of the moon. In the subsequent speech, Lysander's wooing of Hermia is said to have taken place by moonlight. The change that turns Hermia away from her father, and ultimately from Athens, occurs by moonlight.

The complaint Egeus makes is that Hermia refuses to marry Demetrius. Demetrius has won the father's consent to marry, but not the daughter's, for Hermia has fallen in love with Lysander, who has wooed her with rhymes. We have just been told of Theseus's mode of wooing, which has been with the sword and not with rhymes. Unlike Theseus's, Lysander's wooing is said to be all "with feigning voice," singing "feigning verses" by moonlight. The difference between the two modes is perhaps that Hermia is now put into danger of death.

Egeus demands the "ancient privilege" of Athens, which is to dispose of his daughter as he sees fit. The power of the father is unlimited; he is as a god to his child. The power of the father is like that of an artist over his work. He may dispose of his work as he pleases, figure or disfigure as he wills. Is this how the ancient law understands the relationship between the gods and human beings? We shall leave this question aside for the moment for a more immediate one. How much can a father in fact be an artist? Can he really claim to have shaped the child as an artist shapes his work?

The rebellion of Hermia indicates that there is another source which has shaped her. That is the meaning of the accusation of bewitchment or enchantment. Lysander has corrupted the heart of Hermia and changed her into another Hermia, not the one which the father believed he had shaped. The question Theseus faces at the beginning is whether or not another source of shaping the young is to be permitted, or only the power of the father is to be permitted. We see that the city, which is to say, Theseus, is as yet not the authority which claims to be able to shape the souls of the Athenians. For we do know that a city does claim the power to figure or disfigure. But we are still in a prepolitical time; not the city of Theseus, but the father is the shaper of souls. For Theseus to rule, the rule of Egeus must indeed be set aside.

The principal issue at the beginning, then, is the confrontation with the harshness of the ancient law. We see the difficulty with the law when we ask the question, How far is the father in fact an artist? (Locke asks the same question of Sir Robert Filmer in the *First Treatise of Government,* pointing out that the act of begetting can scarcely be likened to making.) The immediate situation is that the law prevents the union of Lysander and Hermia, whose love, nourished as it is by another authority, cannot be consummated in Athens. If Hermia-Lysander and Helena-Demetrius are the proper pairings, then the law is an obstacle to what is fitting. The question, in its extended form, is of course a familiar one: To what extent can the legal and the natural coincide? It appears as if the legal or the conventional are always, if not at odds one with another, then somehow never fully in conjunction with one another. When Demetrius says at the end that he has returned to his "natural taste," does it not mean that now the natural pairings may occur? The fairy charm, therefore, permits the legal and the natural to coincide.

Theseus first attempts to persuade Hermia to obey her father. Why should she not? She owes what she is to her father, and Demetrius is a worthy gentleman. When Hermia replies that Lysander is equal to Demetrius, Theseus declares that while this may be so, the father's voice declares otherwise. Demetrius and Lysander are made unequal by the law. We are reminded that a distinction is always made between citizen and alien, at times on no better basis than the distinction made between Demetrius and Lysander. One has the voice of the city; the other does not.

Hermia wishes that her father could see Lysander with her eyes. The worth of Lysander is seen by Hermia, but she is forbidden to see it because she must see with the judgment, the voice of her father. The eye must see according to the voice; one must wonder if one difficulty with the law is that it deprives the senses of their proper function. Bottom is not the only one in the play to confuse the functions of the senses. The law subordinates sight to another sense, and the eye must, as it were, hear.

Hermia claims to see better than her father, or better than the law. But we remember that according to Egeus, Hermia began to see differently only when Lysander sang feigning verses with feigning voice. Does she not then see also with the voice? She admits later in the scene that Athens, before she loved Lysander, was to her like a paradise. She now sees it as cruel and harsh, a place from which to flee. She had been a happy daughter until she saw with different eyes. Or have the verses permitted her in truth to see more fully? Hermia and Lysander begin with poetry, but they finally claim that their love is the proper, natural one. The love stories they tell each other permit a union which is by nature, instead of simply by law.

Not even Theseus can now persuade or overawe Hermia. She confesses that she is bold, but by what power she knows not. Is it the power of the verses that have captured her imagination? She asks Theseus what her choices are and is given two alternatives, either to die or become a nun. Egeus had mentioned only death. Is the alternative to death offered by Theseus an invention? Has he discovered or pretended to discover some other ancient law? Theseus seems to dwell upon the second choice of Hermia's becoming a nun (why not a priestess?) dedicated to the "cold fruitless moon." It seems odd that Shakespeare should choose to speak of a votary of Artemis or Diana as a nun and a sister. But if the moon has before been connected with the changes in human relationships, it is now said to be barren and cold, the opposite of love. Why, then, should the changes human beings undergo be subject to that which is antierotic? Theseus claims that obedience to the law will bring life among men, love and fruitfulness; disobedience to the law is to become an outcast and be doomed to barrenness and withering. The moon and the city appear to be at odds one with another; one appears as a nonhuman horizon. Does the moon then rule that which is outside the city? Thus, the changes wrought in human beings by the moon would be seen as dangerous to the city and to the laws.

Is Lysander's poetry somehow like the moon because it seems to have its source outside of the city? It belongs then to the moonlit realm, the realm outside the walls or horizon of the city.

Theseus gives Hermia until his wedding day to reflect upon her three choices—death, marriage, or a single life. One can scarcely believe, of course, that the king who wished for nothing but merriment on his wedding day would permit an execution to shadow it. Two of these choices, death or marriage, to repeat, are the choices of her father. The possibility of a single life that is not of the city and is yet suggested by the city is one given by Theseus. Should that possibility exist at all? Can a city permit that possibility to exist? Or does piety always require that possibility to exist? The rational mind, in the sense of the legalistic mind, will not permit the third choice, of a life outside of the city, but a pious man must insist upon it.

Demetrius appeals to Lysander to give up his "crazèd right," and Lysander replies that Demetrius should marry Egeus. The "crazed right" must be the right that love confers. Lysander's reply is an affirmation of his "right," which, then, has also conferred upon Demetrius the right to Egeus.

A new issue is brought up by Lysander. Demetrius made love to Helena and won her, but has now abandoned her. Love not only confers rights, it necessarily brings on obligations. Such obligations must be taken seriously, as Theseus admits. He had heard of the affair, and would have spoken to Demetrius about it had he not been so full of his own affairs. Did Theseus thereby lose an important opportunity to avoid the difficulties he now faces? But Hermia is warned once again to fit her fancies to her father's will. Theseus declares that he cannot extenuate the penalty of the law. He then indicates that he has need of Egeus and Demetrius for something concerning the nuptials. Are they too important to Theseus and Athens simply to be overruled?

III

Hermia and Lysander, now left alone, exchange stories of lovers who come to woe. They comfort themselves with the thought that "the course of true love never did run smooth." Their desperate situation affirms the truth of their love, so every tale and history they have read tells them. The stories of true love they tell each other all have to do with the attraction one to another of those who for one cause or another are unsuitably matched or placed in some difficult circumstance. But does true love never occur between those suitably matched or those who are fortunate? If that were true, there would then be no story. And it is at this point one sees that there is surely something questionable about being guided by stories rather than by laws. We see what the difficulty with poetry is. A story about the fortunate and the suitable is no story. Poetry, having to charm the passions, must speak of the passionate and dramatic. Can the simple and orderly ever be found in poetry? Can happiness and good fortune ever be a good story? And can the decent lives of decent men and women ever make good poetry? The most fundamental criticism of poetry is, therefore, that it cannot present the highest of human things. The familiar way of stating this difficulty is to say that the life of reason or contemplation cannot be represented by the poet. One can further make the point by saying that the happy life as such, whatever it includes, cannot, it would seem, be the subject of poetry. We are thus left wondering if Demetrius is not right in speaking of Lysander's wooing as "crazèd," i.e., cracked or flawed.

We subsequently see how fickle human affections and vows appear to be. To those who know nothing of the fairies, and the lovers in the woods do not see them, what is experienced are sudden and inexplicable changes of faith and affection, changes which occur without apparent causes. There are misapprehensions, misunderstandings, deceit, quarrels, and, finally, violence and the threat of death. We who see the fairies are protected from the pain of such experiences, but we must always keep in mind that the lovers in the play are not. Whatever brings about these inexplicable changes, we do know that the law is a more certain guide than personal and private affection. We do not know and cannot know whether the love between Hermia and Lysander is, as the father says, a temporary fancy. It is obviously safer for the family, for the city, and for Hermia, to guide her affection according to the law and not according to rhymes, conceits, or stories that cannot but be suspect in their one-sided presentation of human things. There is something very bewitching about rhymes and conceits, but are they not illusory?

Lysander determines to flee Athens. The corruption of the young by poetry finally estranges them. Hermia swears to meet him in the woods, and she swears not by love but by the signs of love, which, however, are not a good augury of faithfulness, ending as they do with the fire that burns Dido and with the false vows of men. The inconstancy, brevity, variability, and irrationality of love are made even more vivid by Helena's entrance with her complaints. Helena seems to blame Hermia for attracting Demetrius's love but wishes to become Hermia, but for unclear reasons. As Helena says at the end of the scene:

> Through Athens I am thought as fair as she.
> But what of that? Demetrius thinks not so . . .
> He will not know what all but he do know.
>
> [1.1.227–29]

Hermia is, in fact, the darker of the two. Lysander later calls her an "Ethiope" and a "tawny Tartar" (3.2.257,263). Hermia's open rejection of Demetrius does not suffice for Helena, for it has no effect upon Demetrius, and so Hermia finds it necessary to tell of the planned flight from Athens. Lysander unfolds the exact plan of escape, which proves to be dangerous. The flight is to take place in moonlight, and that is of course impossible if the new moon is four days away, as Hippolyta has told us. But once again a change is related to the moon. Why does Helena decide to tell Demetrius of Hermia's flight? She knows he will pursue her and she hopes, strangely enough, to receive some thanks for this betrayal of her friend. But if Demetrius is able to prevent the escape then she only makes more probable the marriage between Demetrius and Hermia. She seems to be willing to suffer this pain to prove her complete loyalty and subjection to Demetrius's every wish. She herself says that she is a spaniel who fawns on him.

In her speech, she claims that Demetrius errs in doting on Hermia's eyes, but she admits that she does the same in doting on Demetrius. All the lovers are under some delusion. The law can neither do anything to correct the mistaken love of Demetrius nor persuade Hermia and Lysander. Although the law claims that Egeus has judgment, he judges for Demetrius, who is correctly said to be mistaken in his love. The law, therefore, makes Demetrius worse and not better. Indeed the law is of no help to any of the young lovers.

The delusion of lovers, as Helena says, is caused by love's transforming things as it looks to the image in the mind, identifying whatever object it somehow fixes upon as one with the image cherished. The judgment made by love is hasty; why Hermia and not Helena should have been fixed upon appears to be a matter of chance. What occurs to the lovers in the woods illustrates how the affections seem wholly to be subject to chance. Love sees, then, according to a predisposed structure of images; it does not or cannot see with its own eyes but with what must be called the eye of the mind. And how are these images, which the mind sees, made? Are they not formed by such stories as Hermia and Lysander tell each other?

IV

In the second scene of act 1, the craftsmen of Athens gather to prepare a play for the Duke's wedding festivities. Although they are very English workmen, as has been much remarked upon, we are nevertheless reminded of the importance of craftsmen in Athens. In his "Life of Theseus," Plutarch describes how Theseus established the foundations of Athenian democracy, giving to the people an importance they had in no other city. And Plutarch reports that Pericles made "the mechanic multitude" fully a part of the city by establishing a great public works program to adorn and beautify the city.[12] The "mechanicals" of Athens are given a concern for the beautiful, and we ought not be surprised that Peter Quince, Bottom, and their companions reveal an interest in the dramatic craft. The craftsmen of Athens do not mind their own business, as Bottom perfectly illustrates. We know of course that in the festivals of Dionysus in Athens the people were educated in all the forms of poetry. The beginning of such a concern is to be traced back to Theseus. Shakespeare seems to understand this, for his Theseus, against Hippolyta's and Philostrate's (or Egeus's) protests,[13] insists on choosing to hear the play of

> Hard-handed men that work in Athens here,
> Which never labored in their minds till now;
> And now have toiled their unbreathed memories. . . .
> [5.1.72–74]

Athens is a city wholly informed by poetry, where even the "shallowest thickskin" may pretend to mastery in poetics.

The play the craftsmen prepare is to be a lamentable comedy of a cruel death, thus mixing comedy and tragedy into one work. One wonders if the "intents" of the craftsmen, "Extremely stretched, and conned with cruel pain," as they are, are directed toward putting on the most perfect drama possible. A lamentable comedy or a comical tragedy is, of course, an oxymoron, a seeming impossibility, yet the most perfect representation of the human condition might be the death of a lover in what is at the same time a comedy. And if writing both comedies and tragedies might be said to be the highest aspiration of the playwright, what of writing a tragic comedy?

When Bottom is told that he is to play Pyramus, he immediately wants to know if Pyramus is a lover or a tyrant. It would seem that a play could only present one or the other. Only lovers and tyrants can appear in poetry. When Quince answers that Pyramus is a lover who kills himself, Bottom declares that he prefers to play a tyrant. A lover makes one weep, but a tyrant is fearful and lofty. To make men fearful is loftier than to make them weep storms of tears. Bottom illustrates the point by reciting some lofty verses, spoken by Heracles, in which Phoebus Apollo is said to mar, i.e., conquer, the foolish fates. The reference seems to be to Aeschylus's *Oresteia,* in which Apollo helps to balk the Furies of their revenge upon Orestes. Bottom prefers his genres pure and not mixed. He wants a tragedy that will represent a tyrant. A lover is more "condoling," says Bottom, i.e., more giving of sympathetic sorrowing, but is he not more passive, accepting and not marring what the fates do?

Quince simply ignores Bottom's ranting and goes on calling the roll of players and giving them parts they are to play. Bottom, like a tyrant, wishes to play every part except those of the mother and father, and these are later dropped from the play. He especially likes the role of the lion, which, everyone fears, will frighten the ladies and make the Duke hang the actors. Something must therefore be done to indicate that the lion is not truly a lion and its part must be made more gentle. Thus the first difficulty the amateur players meet concerns the limitations imposed on what can be presented on the stage. These limitations, however, are imposed by the passions of the audience and not by any difficulties inherent in stagecraft itself. The Athenian mechanicals are careful about the effect of their representations upon the passions of the audience, especially the passions of the women, but it is because they fear hanging. Bottom wants his effects to impress the Duke, but Quince reminds him that he cannot carry his effects too far. Fear of the Duke seems to be a salutary limitation to the desire of a Bottom to roar as terribly as he can. But if a lion in a play must not be as terrible as is the lion itself, one wonders if the roles of tyrant and lover must also be moderated. Must the tyrant be made less fearful and the lover less condoling?

V

We are now introduced to fairyland, and the speaker is Puck. We quickly learn that there is a division in fairyland between the King and the Queen. Titania, the Queen, has a child that Oberon, the King, desires but which is refused him. Puck speaks of the child as stolen from an Indian. Titania speaks later of the boy's mother but never mentions the father.

"Titania" (Titan's daughter) is a name that has given rise to critical speculation.[14] I will only note that there is perhaps some kind of connection between the fairies and the Titans. One possibility, for example, is that the fairies like the Titans are more nearly cosmological gods—gods, i.e., like the Earth, the Sun, and the Moon. As for Oberon, his name recalls the medieval romances, in which tradition he appears as a pre-Christian spirit who yet obeys God and helps the Church.[15]

When Titania and Oberon meet in the moonlight, they accuse each other of various infidelities, including those which involve Hippolyta and Theseus.[16] But Hippolyta and Theseus seem unaware of the existence of the fairies; Theseus, after all, explains away reports of their appearances as mere fancies. And when he speaks of "fairy time," it is evident that he is only using a figure of speech. Could the fairies, however, have appeared in different forms? Or do they remain invisible presences even to those whom they favor?

Titania points out that the discord between the fairy sovereigns has led to a discord in all nature and has affected the lives of human beings. The proper order, concord, and festivities of the fairies keep all nature in harmony. The first effect of the fairy discord is upon air, and then upon water, which turns earth to mud. The disharmony between air and water disturbs all the seasons; fire is prevented from doing its proper work. The moon, therefore, the governor of floods, now rules and not the sun.

It has been noticed that despite Titania's report of bad weather, the weather in the *Dream* is good, permitting lovers and amateur actors to stay outdoors all night in bright moonlight.[17] One wonders if the two worlds, fairy and mortal, quite coincide. More of these curious discrepancies appear later.

Titania can end the disharmony, Oberon replies, by giving him the boy, and once again she vigorously refuses. She loved the boy's mother and will raise him for the sake of the mother. Does the rule of the moon and water also signify the untoward dominance of the female element?[18]

Oberon promises to torment Titania before she leaves the wood. To do this, he sends Puck upon an errand to fetch a herb called love-in-idleness. He reminds Puck of a time when he, Oberon, sat upon a promontory and heard the song of a mermaid. The song made the rude sea orderly but it disordered the stars, making them shoot out from their orbits. The mermaid rides upon a dolphin—both of them are creatures of two realms. The mermaid is half-human and half-animal; the dolphin's leaping from water to air has been taken as a metaphor of the soul that leaps from the mortal body into an immortal realm.

The sublunary region has been thought of as the realm of change or of chance; the celestial spheres above the moon are changeless in their motion and hence are the realm of the rational. The rule of the moon is thus the rule of chance, of the variable and the irrational.[19] The effect of the mermaid's music, then, is to give order to that which is by nature disorderly, and to make the perfectly rational mad and eccentric.

Puck remembers the music. Oberon not only had heard the music, but also had seen Cupid, flying between "the cold moon and the earth." Perhaps maddened by the music, Cupid shoots his love-shaft at a vestal virgin, a priestess of Diana, and the moon quenches the arrow before it strikes, making it fall upon a white flower which then turns purple. The music of the mermaid must somehow be connected with Cupid's firing his bolt. Perhaps in trying to shoot the votaress of Diana he wished to disturb the coldness and freedom from passions of the maiden. Is such coldness the divine imitation, or the imitation of the courses of the heavenly bodies? Cupid would then be emboldened by the mermaid's music, which disturbs the heavenly spheres, also to disturb the consecrated maiden. But he is prevented from committing a sacrilege and the virgin does not notice the attempt; it is not the virgin who is to carry love's wound, but the flower. The flower's juice has now the power of Cupid's arrow. Does the flower also have the power of the mermaid's music? Does eros have the same effect as that music? Music, eros, and the moon are linked together by one thing—they are all connected to metamorphoses. As the mermaid's music changes the motions of the sea and the stars, so does Cupid's arrow change a flower, and the flower's juice will bring about changes in Titania, Lysander, and Demetrius. The moon is of course in constant change, and we have noted that it is in moonlight that changes in human beings take place.

Oberon's plan is to make Titania so infatuated with some vile thing that she will give up the changeling boy. He believes, therefore, that Titania's love for the boy is some kind of delusion. What Oberon effects is what Helena has previously described as the result of the power of love: "Things base and vile, holding no quantity,/Love can transpose to form and dignity" (1.1.232–33). The flower's juice is to make Titania fall in love with something vile, to teach her perhaps that her love for the Indian boy is such a delusion. Titania is too much in love with a mortal, and she is to be taught not to hold mortals so dearly.

The love-juice is placed by mistake upon Lysander's eyes, and upon his seeing Helena he begins to argue like a scholastic. Lysander now claims to see most truly; he has become, he says, completely rational and he therefore no longer speaks like a poet. The flower in fact makes him an angry man; he cries out: "Where is Demetrius? O how fit a word/Is that vile name to perish on my sword" (2.2.106–7). That Demetrius is a brutal man is confirmed by the scene when he is alone with Helena in the woods pursuing Hermia and Lysander. Demetrius, who stands by the law, warns Helena that they are outside the city and his passions are therefore no longer governed by the law. Lysander is now like Demetrius and Egeus, a rational and angry man.

On the other hand, when the love-juice is placed by Oberon on Demetrius's eyes, upon seeing Helena he begins speaking like a poet. He does not do very well, but he certainly sounds better than did before: "O Helen, my goddess, nymph, perfect, divine!/To what my love, shall I compare thine eyne?" (3.2.137–38). The difference between Lysander and Demetrius is clear. Lysander was already under the spell of poetry and did not need the flower's juice; Demetrius required it to dispel his anger and violence. Can Lysander also be said to have been already under the power of eros? Is the flower, therefore, an adequate substitute for poetry? One may be under the delusions induced by music, eros, poetry, or the flower, but are the transformations which these bring about the same? Had Cupid fired his bolt at Demetrius, would he not also have become better?

One notices that even without the intervention of the fairies, human lives are subject to sudden and inexplicable changes. The fairies were not responsible for Demetrius's change toward Helena, or for that matter Hermia's change toward her father and Athens. When Lysander, under the flower's spell, declares himself surfeited with Hermia, he speaks of a most common experience. What makes it uncommon is the speed with which it has occurred. The quarrels among the lovers in the woods are both comic and sad. Sad because the sudden changes of affection are painful, and the mortals in the play have no way of understanding these transformations; Hermia awakes in fear, having had a terrible dream, and finding Lysander gone searches for him in fear and sorrow. Comic because we know that errors in perception are the causes of the quarrels, and we are assured, by seeing the fairies, that these will be rectified.

Mortals are fools, as Puck says, because they so greatly misconceive their own intentions and interests and those of others. They deceive themselves and each other, and that is why

Helena cannot believe in what is professed either by Lysander or Demetrius. The distrust and pain are overcome only when they fall asleep and remember the fairies vaguely, as in a dream.

One also notices that the mortal women do not undergo any changes. They remain fixed in their affections throughout the play. They do not need the potion, but Hermia needs not to rely on human vows, Helena to become less of a spaniel.

Hermia gives up the security of city walls and city law for the sake of Lysander. She believes in his faithfulness and trustworthiness, and she is made to experience the opposite. Helena is even more rash, for she gives herself up completely to a most unreliable man. Hermia and Helena are alike in their dependence; perhaps, then, they assume that no harm will really come to them. What they experience in the woods is the Hobbesian state of nature—of fear and pain, darkness and death. The woods are especially the confrontation with chance, and the women experience a world without love, friendship, or intelligibility. Helena tries to call upon the schoolgirl memories of friendship, but it seems to no avail. Prudence is perhaps what is required in the world of the woods, and prudence is what both women especially lack. Perhaps, however, women never truly see the world as cold, heartless necessity, barren of sentiment, without meaning or order. Men can believe that they see such a world and then declare that they will conquer it. Do women tend to trust that the world has order and purpose? No wonder, then, that neither Hermia nor Helena requires the potion. They need the opposite.

VI

We must turn now to the other humans in the woods that night, the craftsmen of Athens. Of all the mortals, Bottom is the only one who sees the fairies and abides with them. And Bottom, literalist that he is, makes no distinction between the realm of the fairies and the humans. It is he, then, who has "a most rare vision," and that means that the dream is somehow especially his; it is, he declares, to be called *Bottom's Dream.*

To understand Bottom and his dream, we must look at what happens in the rehearsal in the woods. Upon their gathering together, Bottom immediately raises difficulties about the play.

He declares there are some things in the play that cannot please, the first of which is that Pyramus is to kill himself. Snout and Starveling are struck by the objection, but Bottom has a solution. A prologue must be written that will anticipate the objectionable scene, and assurance must be given the audience that no harm will come to anyone. It is especially important the audience be reminded that Pyramus is not Pyramus. Shakespeare himself subsequently takes Bottom's advice when he has Oberon tell us what will happen with the lovers, thus putting us out of fear: "There shall the pairs of faithful lovers be/Wedded, with Theseus in all jollity" (4.1.97–98). We must remember that at this point in the play the difficulty with Egeus has not as yet been overcome, the threat of which reappears in the very next scene (4.2.160–65).

Bottom's suggestion of a prologue is accepted by the rest of the players. He now raises again the difficulty of a lion—a lion also being unpleasant because it causes fear. But he is now more explicit about the solution than he was before, when he was begging for the role. Once again the audience must be assured that they are seeing only similitudes. The image must not be so convincing that one forgets that the lion on the stage is no such thing (3.1.8ff.).

Bottom's concern is always with the effect upon the audience. It is Quince who raises the difficulty of representing moonlight and a wall. Quince's concern is not with the passions of the audience but the more technical one of presenting similitudes upon the stage. Snug wonders if there is to be moonlight on the night they are to present the play, and Bottom leaps in immediately with the helpful suggestion that they look in the almanac to find out. They discover the moon will shine that night, and Bottom suggests using the moonlight itself. Quince counters the proposal by suggesting that someone come in with a bush and lanthorn "to disfigure, or to present, the person of Moonshine" (3.1.51–53).

The question of how one presents the moon may be said to dominate the play.[20] The play opens, we recall, with Theseus and Hippolyta impatiently waiting out the four days before the appearance of the new moon, and yet the night in the woods is flooded with bright moonlight. Moreover, despite the fact that the lovers seem to have spent only one night in the woods, the morning after their adventure Theseus announces that the wedding festivities are to take place that night, although only two days have passed. Nor could it be possible for the moon to shine the night the craftsmen are to present their play.

As we have noted, this confusion of cycles may be found throughout the play. The fairies have flowers of spring and fruits of autumn to offer to Bottom. When Bottom awakes from his vision, it is early morning. But he does not turn up until evening to tell his friends that he somehow knows their play has been chosen by the Duke. One cannot but be amused by Shakespeare's reassurance that he does know how to look up moonshine—one looks in an almanac, and if the ancient Athenians did not have one, he and Bottom certainly do.

Bottom would have the moon itself directly present in the play. But Shakespeare does as Quince suggests and figures and disfigures the moon, representing and misrepresenting it. The power and problematic nature of poetry is thus revealed. Poetry has the power to make us forget that the representation or imitation may even be a distortion of what is. We are, therefore, misled.

The difficulty of representing a wall is also solved by Bottom. A man must represent a wall, and he is to be covered with plaster or loam. We thus see another aspect of the power of images. Human beings can represent everything—beasts, celestial bodies, and walls. Everything natural or made may be imitated; the whole world can be represented by man. It is no wonder that we have spoken so much of transformation and metamorphosis, for man can become all other things.

That Bottom should now be changed or transformed is only fitting. He has just given expert advice on how everything might be presented on stage. What Puck has done is no more than what Bottom did in bringing moonshine itself onto the stage. Bottom is to become the image of himself. The jest is that he is unaware of what has happened. When he becomes the image of himself and sings—the music is again that of the half-human—Titania comes to him saying, "What angel wakes me from my flowery bed?"

Bottom's literalness permits him to enter the fairy world. Entering the fairy world is, then, a metaphor for being one with the world of images, to be utterly enraptured by the representations of things.

The accepted signification of Bottom's name is that it refers to the bottom, or core, of the skein on which the weaver winds the yarn. The obvious connection between the name and with his being, literally, an ass must not, however, be overlooked. If by entering the fairy world the dream of a Midsummer Night might be said to be Bottom's Dream, then it is a dream of the fool whose body is all too heavily present.

It would seem appropriate that Bottom the weaver, who is an ass and is duly transformed into one, should be the one who weaves together the various worlds of the play.[21] We note also that the gross and palpable devices Bottom suggests are, with one exception, the very ones used to beguile us.

When we return to the question of what is a Midsummer Night's dream, we shall have to reply that the dreams reported by Bottom and the lovers have something ambiguous about them. We are not certain what has occurred. Only one dream has in fact been dreamt in the woods—Hermia's nightmare. Bottom and the lovers alike remember the events of the night as if they were dreams. When Puck speaks of the entire play as dream, he thus puts us in the same situation as those who had been in the woods. We look back at what we have experienced as if it were a dream. We should also note that the craftsmen believe that something *has* happened to Bottom;[22] what has gone on in the woods is not a dream to them. A midsummer night's dream is one that cannot simply be said to be the result of fancies brought about by fear and hope. Such a dream, one might say, has its own independent life, as do the fairy realm and the play.

Bottom knows that it is "past the wit of man to say what dream it was" that he has had, and he also knows that it should only be presented as a ballad. Professor Richard H. Cox has pointed out that Bottom's account of his dream is a parody of 1 Corinthians 2.9, one of the New Testament's most important treatments of the tension between philosophy and revelation. Professor Cox then suggests that Bottom substitutes the things which have occurred in the woods for revelation.[23]

We do notice that the lovers wander in darkness and then fall into deep deathlike sleep before they are awakened to a new life by the horns of Theseus. Bottom is spoken of as having been "transported" by the craftsmen, and it has been noted that "transported" is a euphemism for dying, and is so used elsewhere by Shakespeare.[24] What is important, however, is the effect of the dreams upon the mortals. Hermia puts it best. Upon waking, she exclaims that she sees as if things were double. The dreamers see not one world but two, and this seeing remains with them.

In Plato's *Republic,* dreaming is described as "believing a likeness of something to be not a likeness, but rather the thing itself to which it is like."[25] Such is surely the condition of Bottom, and of Demetrius who does not know how truly he speaks when he says, "It seems to be, / That yet we sleep, we dream." The ordinary man, it is said in the *Republic,* is law-abiding while awake, but when he goes to sleep he also puts to sleep "the calculating, tame, and ruling part" of his soul, "while the beastly and wild part, gorged with food and drink," awakens and dreams of doing everything without shame and without prudence. But the good man, as distinguished from the ordinary man, knows how to moderate the desiring and spirited parts of his soul, and sets his rational part in motion before he sleeps. Such a man has fair dreams, and "in such a state he most lays hold of the truth"[26] The good man's dream is like a vision of the good.[27] But what the ordinary man only dreams of, the tyrant dares to do awake. Are we meant, then, to think of the counterpart of the tyrant, i.e., the one who sees while awake what the good man can only lay hold of in dreams? Is the counterpart of the tyrant then the philosopher? The actualization of dreams or the bringing of dreams into the awake life would then be the work of the tyrant and the philosopher.

Does *A Midsummer Night's Dream* reveal the nature of the good man's dream? The blessing given at the end of the play would indicate that it does. The dream, then, that belongs to the shortest night of the year is the vision of the good. The *Dream* given to us is one of a fairy concord that removes "all the blots of Nature's hand." It is the dream of Nature given a completeness it otherwise, perhaps, does not have. The potion or the poem or the song provides the dimly remembered experience of the fairies who give significance, i.e., intelligibility, to the changes that afflict human beings, changes which would otherwise be either inexplicable or else, without the dream, would be too cruel or too hard to speak of.

The dream replaces the harshness of the law. The fairies bring together the couples who were kept apart by the laws of the city. We have also seen that what the law could not do with Demetrius is done by the potion. The fairies' blessing of Theseus's household also suggests that what the law could not properly order is made possible by the fairies or the *Dream.*

We know, of course, of the polemic waged against the poets throughout the *Republic*. In what way is the poet different from the tyrant or philosopher? Is he also an awake man? From the discussion in the *Republic* it would seem that the poets do not understand, and therefore only the philosophic man can truly be a poet—a maker who correctly imitates those things that are.

In writing *A Midsummer Night's Dream,* Shakespeare reveals that at least one poet is able to present the dream which good men dream, the one that corresponds to the vision of the good. Shakespeare is the philosophic poet who, unlike Bottom, is aware of what he sees. Shakespeare has made a similitude which while it puts us under a spell reminds us at the same time that it is only a similitude. We dream, but it is a dream that is like being awake, and thus a dream for the shortest night of the year when darkness and sleep are least.

Oberon, at the darkest time of the play both literally and metaphorically, is warned of the coming dawn. He is called king of the shadows, and the fairies usually do follow the darkness as it circles the globe. Oberon says, however, that the fairies are not like ghosts who fear the morning sun. The shadows of which Puck speaks are to be found in churchyards; they are shadows from the afterlife. According to Oberon, the fairies have nothing to do with ghosts or the afterlife. Does this mean they have nothing to do with questions of judgment, salvation, and damnation?

VII

Theseus, in reflecting upon the accounts of the lovers, declares his skepticism of the visions in the woods. He believes that all such are fantasies, the result of either desire or fear. Hippolyta, in contrast, insists that if a story "grows to something of great constancy," it must be so, no matter how "strange and admirable." And yet the law itself is some such delusion, as we have seen at the beginning. Is not Theseus, however, simply mistaken? We have seen that there is something more to the fairies than either fear or hope. When he defends his choice of the craftsmen's play to Hippolyta, he seems to regard the performance of plays as something that ought to be done, as a sign of "a rationally stabilized commonwealth." His attitude toward poetry seems to be entirely manipulative or, as has been said, "administrative."[28]

But to accept the stories told by the lovers, as Hippolyta does, as something more than fancy, would be to make literal what cannot be but as a likeness or a metaphor. Hippolyta would have us see with a single eye, and not with Hermia's double vision. To see with a single eye would be like Bottom's using moonshine to represent itself. Theseus is cautious of the power of the imagination—as is Socrates and, we have argued, Shakespeare himself. Those who would take Hippolyta's view,[29] and these are many, wish to fall wholly under the charm of the imagination. Hippolyta proves Theseus to be right when he says that "Such tricks hath strong imagination, / That if it would apprehend some joy, / It comprehends some bringer of that job" (5.1.18–20).

The play the Athenian craftsmen put on is a working out of what a play should be, or how poetry should be permitted to exist in the city. It is, as Theseus says, a "palpable gross play," and yet it has beguiled the night. Shakespeare appears always to have something in his plays by which the spell of the illusions we are witnessing is broken. Even so gross a play as that of *Pyramus and Thisbe* seems to be able to touch those who hear it. Theseus, after Pyramus's speech bewailing Thisbe's supposed death, remarks: "This passion, and the death of a dear friend, / Would go near to make a man look sad" (5.1.281), to which the Duchess replies "Beshrew my heart, but I pity the man." In other words, such a scene in more skillful hands would indeed make men weep.

We now see the resolution of how the moon is to be represented. As Wall is personified, so is the moon—by a man with a lanthorn, thornbush, and dog. Unlike Wall, however, who is covered with lime and hair, it is difficult immediately to see that a man with such appurtenances signifies the moon or moonshine. Theseus declares this representation to be "the greatest error of all the rest." The four-part image—man, dog, bush, lanthorn—represents not the moon but the man in the moon with his bush and dog. The craftsmen err by being too literal, and the ducal audience is therefore moved to criticize the image as defective in its literalness: the man, dog, and bush should be in the lanthorn. Shakespeare has already shown there is no need for such devices; he has made us see the moon in all its phases (waning, full, new) at his will. But is it not better than the literalness of the craftsmen be made grossly obvious? Hippolyta's literalism is a more dangerous one, because it does not express itself in such evident devices. She, and those like her, therefore, fall prey to the devices of the poet, which are worked out only in speech.

To see double is to see metaphorically: to be and not be at one and the same time. And one cannot see double unless there is such a poet as Shakespeare who knows how to apply and remove the potion.

VIII

The effect of poetry upon the human being is the same as that of the flower's juice. Those who have been touched by poetry have no need of fairy power or magic. *A Midsummer Night's Dream* also suggests that the work of eros is done through poetry. Demetrius seems impervious to poetry and eros. He is one of those violent men, "stockish, hard, and full of rage," whose soul is not moved by the "concord of sweet sounds." Hence it is necessary that Oberon intervene and apply the flower juice to his eyes. Poetry does not touch all men's souls; something else must be done with Demetrius, and that something else is the fairy world. The conversion of a Demetrius cannot perhaps be done by simply human means. In *As You Like It,* the evil brothers are suddenly and miraculously converted from their wicked ways. Thus the flower and the fairies represent the possibility of such conversion, for unless this possibility exists, one could not believe in the existence of a beneficent nature as is promised in the blessing of the fairies:

> Now until the break of day,
> Through this house each Fairy stray.
> To the best Bride-bed will we,
> Which by us shall blessed be:
> And the issue there create,
> Ever shall be fortunate:
> So shall all the couples three,
> Ever true in loving be:
> And the blots of Nature's hand,
> Shall not in their issue stand.
> Never mole, harelip, nor scar,
> Nor mark prodigious, such as are
> Despised in Nativity,
> Shall upon their children be.
>
> [5.1.390–403]

Nature has "blots" and "prodigies" that require amending. Nature is thus not wholly beneficent in and of itself, but it is the fairies who give the possibility of amendment.

The rule of Theseus depends upon the fairy blessing. We are told by Aristotle that kingship depends upon the supposition that nature is beneficent. That is because the rule of a king is more like the rule of the master or father of a household than all other forms of political rule. Hence he depends less upon the law and more upon this particular or personal relationship with each of his subjects. The existence of a natural order, or the belief in the existence of such an order, is therefore necessary for a king. He must have the souls of his subjects shaped by an order that exists outside the laws of the city. Thus the insufficiencies of the laws of Athens must be made up by the ordering or blessing of the household by the fairies.

We should consider, however, that other aspect of Athens which, according to Plutarch, existed with the founding of the city by Theseus, and that is her democratic tendencies. We have seen that the dream vision affects all classes, and that the commons are to be stretched beyond their limits to share in what Athens is to be. Theseus argues against Hippolyta that whatever the people cannot do, whatever is lacking, must be supplied. Is too much given here to poetry? For it seems to be expected that poetry will make possible a new kind of equality or friendship among the citizens. The dream vision of the fairies, who amend the defects of nature, would seem especially to be the yearning or dream of the animate body—which is to say, of Bottom. It is the fulfillment of this dream in and through poetry, making of Bottom a prince consort, which finally seems to permit the people to become fully a part of the city.

In *Timon of Athens,* we learn that Athens is the city dedicated to the beautiful and that means dedicated to the removal of the necessitous. Timon is presented as the man who especially gives himself to the task of transforming the city into a thing of love and beauty, where citizenship is a communion of friends who give freely one to another. One sees in Timon the complete forgetfulness of "the blots of Nature" that can be induced by the love of the beautiful—the forgetfulness, that is to say, of the difference between the beautiful similitude and what it imitates. Poetry may have replaced revelation in Athens, but it brings along with it new dangers. In *Timon,* Athens has abandoned the political, believing itself to be a city transformed or transported. But as that last word implies, such a city is dead. Timon's last act is to bury himself, leaving an epitaph as a memorial.[30]

In *A Midsummer Night's Dream,* however, we are at the origins of that city, and we should be left with the memory not of decay and death but of the freshness of things. We should return, like Hermia, to Athens, once more seeing it as a Paradise.

Notes

1. That *A Midsummer Night's Dream* is concerned with the founding of Athens was first suggested to me by Howard B. White in *Copp'd Hills Towards Heaven: Shakespeare and the Classical Polity* (The Hague: Martinus Nijhoff, 1970), p. 46.

2. See Ralph Berry, *Shakespeare's Comedies: Explorations in Form* (Princeton, N.J.: Princeton University Press, 1972), p. 89; Marjorie B. Garber, *Dream in Shakespeare. From Metaphor to Metamorphosis* (New Haven, Conn.: Yale University Press, 1974), p. 77; David P. Young, *Something of Great Constancy. The Art of "A Midsummer Night's Dream"* (New Haven, Conn.: Yale University Press, 1966), pp. 125–26.

3. Except, possibly, for *The Tempest.* See Sheldon P. Zitner, "The Worlds of *A Midsummer Night's Dream,*" *South Atlantic Quarterly* 59 (1960): 398; C. L. Barber, *Shakespeare's Festive Comedy* (Princeton, N.J.: Princeton University Press, 1959), pp. 147–48.

4. Ernest Schanzer, "The Central Theme of *A Midsummer Night's Dream,*" *University of Toronto Quarterly* 20 (1951): 232–33.

5. 1.1.165–67; 4.1.131–33. Line citations follow the Penguin edition of Shakespeare's *Complete Works,* ed. Alfred Harbage (New York: Viking, 1969).

6. See also Barber, *Shakespeare's Festive Comedy,* pp. 120–21.

7. Ibid., pp. 123–24, 144–45; Roger Lancelyn Green, "Shakespeare and the Fairies," *Folklore* 73 (1962): 89–103. Cf. Peter F. Fisher, "The Argument of *A Midsummer Night's Dream,*" *Shakespeare Quarterly* 8 (1957): 307–8.

8. Plutarch, *The Lives of the Noble Grecians and Romans,* trans. John Dryden, rev. Arthur Hugh Clough (New York: The Modern Library, n.d.), pp. 5, 15, 16.

9. I owe the interpretation of the program of sculptures of the Parthenon to a lecture given by Peter H. von Blanckenhagen. See also Martin Robertson and Alison Frantz, *The Parthenon Frieze* (New York: Oxford University Press, 1975), p. 8. Cf. P. E. Corbett, *The Sculpture of the Parthenon* (Harmondsworth: Penguin Books, 1959), pp. 12, 34n.6.

10. Plutarch, *Lives,* p. 48.

11. Richard H. Cox points out that there are 46 uses of words referring to the moon: there are 31 references to the moon, 1 to moonbeams, 6 to moonlight, and 8 to moonshine. "Shakespeare: Poetic Understanding and Comic Action. A Weaver's Dream," in *The Artist and Political Vision,* ed. Benjamin R. Barber and Michael J. Gargar McGrath (New Brunswick, N.J.: Transaction Books, 1982), p. 176. See also Ernest Schanzer, "The Moon and the Fairies in *A Midsummer Night's Dream,*" *University of Toronto Quarterly* 24 (1955): 241, 243–44; Barber, *Shakespeare's Festive Comedy,* p. 149; White, *Copp'd Hills,* pp. 51–52.

12. Plutarch, *Lives,* p. 192.

13. The text of the First Folio has Egeus speaking the lines; the Quartos have Philostrate. See *A New Variorum Edition of Shakespeare. A Midsummer Night's Dream,* ed. Howard H. Furness (New York: Dover, 1963).

14. See Schanzer, "The Moon and the Fairies," p. 241; Green, "Shakespeare and the Fairies," pp. 91–93; E. K. Chambers, *Shakespeare: A Survey* (New York: Hill & Wang, n.d.), pp. 77–78; Paul A. Olson, "*A Midsummer Night's Dream* and the Meaning of Court Marriage," *Journal of English Literary History* 24 (1957): 109–11.

15. Olson, "Meaning of Court Marriage," pp. 109–11; T. Walter Herbert, *Oberon's Mazèd World* (Baton Rouge, La.: Louisiana State University Press, 1977), p. 38.

16. E. C. Pettet, *Shakespeare and the Romance Tradition* (London: Staples Press, 1949), p. 112; G. Wilson Knight, *The Shakespearean Tempest* (London: Methuen, 1932), p. 167.

17. Herbert, *Oberon's Mazèd World,* pp. 153–54.

18. Olson, "Meaning of Court Marriage," pp. 102–3.

19. White, *Copp'd Hills,* p. 51, points out that the sublunary world is the political world.

20. See Barber, *Shakespeare's Festive Comedy,* pp. 148–50, and, especially, Cox, "Shakespeare: Poetic Understanding," pp. 185–86.

21. William B. Dillingham, "Bottom: The Third Ingredient," *Emory University Quarterly* 12 (1956): 230–37.

22. 4.2.1ff.

23. But see Robert F. Willson, Jr., "God's Secrets and Bottom's Name: A Reply," *Shakespeare Quarterly* 20 (1979): 407–8, and J. Dennis Huston, "Bottom Waking: Shakespeare's 'Most Rare Vision,'" *Studies in English Literature* 13 (1974): 212, who deny that there is any religious significance to Bottom's remarks. Cf. T. M. Pearce, "*MND,* IV, i, 214–215," *Explicator* 18 (1959).

24. See the *New Variorum Edition. A Midsummer Night's Dream,* p. 196, n. 5.

25. Plato, *The Republic,* trans. Allan Bloom (New York: Basic Books, 1968), 476c–d.

26. ". . . and the sights that are hostile to law show up least in his dreams." Ibid., 571c–572a.

27. Ibid., 534c.

28. Howard Nemerov, "The Marriage of Theseus and Hippolyta," *Kenyon Review* 18 (1956): 636; Robert Crossley, "Education and Fantasy," *College English* 37 (1975): 285, is especially harsh: "He [Theseus] is the ass, the patched fool, the man of truncated wisdom and practical discretions."

29. See J. A. Bryant, Jr., *Hippolyta's View. Some Christian Aspects of Shakespeare's Plays* (Lexington, Ky.: University of Kentucky Press, 1961), p. 3.

30. This interpretation is further worked out in my essay, "Timon of Athens," in *Shakespeare as a Political Thinker,* ed. John E. Alvis and Thomas G. West (Durham, N.C.: Carolina Academic Press, 1981).

Hugh MacDiarmid and the Lenin/Douglas Line

Stephen P. Smith

Idaho State University

WHEN Hugh MacDiarmid, the leading literary figure of the Scottish Renaissance Movement of the 1920s and 1930s, began writing poems in Synthetic Scots—an amalgamation of the language of Dunbar and various modern Scots dialects—he emerged as both a poet of great technical virtuosity and as a spokesman for Scotland's nationalist aspirations. For MacDiarmid, the revival of Scots as a literary language was necessary not only for his development as a poet but for the political struggle with England. As part of the cultural awakening of the Scottish Renaissance, the return to Scots provides the nationalist movement with one more weapon to fight the central government and the "sinister little Tory-Socialist alliances of all kinds"[1] that resist the revolutionary movement. However, MacDiarmid's political views, both with respect to his espousal of Communism and the larger issue of the Pan-Celtic Front, have quite naturally led to two basic misunderstandings. The first neatly divides MacDiarmid's thought into three distinct periods, each of which negates or assimilates the preceding. Thus, Duncan Glen implies that MacDiarmid's evolution as a political poet involves phases as a Nationalist, a Communist, and, finally, a Pan-Celtist.[2] The second misunderstanding paints MacDiarmid as so unorthodox and eccentric a Communist that, as David Craig maintains, "it is surely in his poetry, and nowhere else, that his Marxism lies," for "if we consider MacDiarmid's Communism as a body of opinions, the inconsistencies typical of his thinking are as crippling there as anywhere."[3] MacDiarmid himself adds to the confusion by his avowed dissociation from certain elements of the nationalist movement and by comments like the following in his autobiography: "But the trouble in my case is rather that I have always been . . . 'an Anarchist of course'. . . . Communism is a stage on the way to Anarchism—a necessary and indispensable stage; the only entrance to the promised land."[4] However, this concept of Communism is more orthodox than it may at first appear. Indeed, a continuity of thought, identified by Sydney Goodsir Smith as the John Maclean Communist line,[5] does run through the prose and poetry of MacDiarmid. But it is, more accurately, the Lenin/Douglas line that forms the basis of MacDiarmid's political and economic ideas.

The seemingly irreconcilable causes of Communism and Scottish Nationalism are not merely further examples of MacDiarmid's faith in the fundamental contrarieties of the Scottish mind, although Sydney Goodsir Smith treats them as such. After quoting from a 1945 essay by MacDiarmid, Smith explains its defense of a uniquely Scottish Communism with the aesthetic loophole that "the inconsistencies of an artist are essential to his nature."[6] The quotation in question, which originally appeared in the *Scots Independent,* is important to consider in full:

> I write as a Scottish Communist. These words mean exactly what they say. They do not mean Russian Communist. Russia stands at a very different stage of development from Scotland, and has a very different historical background. My Russian comrades can get on with their own affairs. I, on the other hand, am almost exclusively concerned with Scotland. The application of Communism in any country depends upon the accurate analysis of all the elements in its economic, political, cultural and social position and potentialities in the light of Dialectical Materialism. I accept that method of interpreting history, but I personally do not feel qualified to apply it myself to any country but Scotland, the only country of which I have the necessary first-hand knowledge and into whose problems and potentialities I have made the necessary intensive and comprehensive research.[7]

The fact that the Communist Party of Great Britain at one time expelled MacDiarmid for this "unorthodox" nationalism proves only the extent to which party members had failed to understand Lenin. In fact, MacDiarmid's nationalist ideas coincide perfectly with Lenin's own writings about the nationalist question, a fact which MacDiarmid returns to in his discussion of John Maclean in *The Company I've Kept:* "Lenin's view was that national emancipation struggles were a necessary preliminary to the successful waging of the class struggle within the freed nations."[8] The theme of both the *Scots Independent* article and the essay on Maclean—that Scotland can and should develop, along nationalist lines, a unique brand of Communism—can be found in the writings of Lenin himself.

Only recently has Lenin's prominence as a theorist as well as a man of shrewd political action been adequately recognized. In his introduction to a selection of Lenin's political writings, James E. Connor points out that Lenin's theoretical revisions of basic Marxist doctrine regarding the international socialist movement made possible the revolutionary impetus that Communism became to nationalist movements around the world.[9] Rejecting the Marxist view that nationalist movements were bourgeois disguises meant to conceal the true class structure of the state, Lenin transformed Marxism into a pragmatic plan of action through which individual nations might plot their own futures. Georg Lukács had noted the antidogmatic stance of Lenin's revisionist theories as early as 1924, writing that "Leninism represents a hitherto unprecedented degree of concrete, unschematic, unmechanistic, purely praxis-oriented thought."[10] On the national question, Lenin is particularly "concrete, unschematic, unmechanistic." In 1899, early in his theoretical development, Lenin writes in *Our Program* that "this theory [Marxism] provides only the general guiding principles which in *detail* must be applied in England in a manner different from that applied in France, in France in a manner different from that applied in Germany, and in Germany in a manner different from that applied in Russia."[11] As a class movement, nationalist struggles for independence are, as they are for MacDiarmid, necessary stages in the dialectical progress of society; in 1914, Lenin writes in *Karl Marx:* "The nation is a necessary product, an inevitable form, in the bourgeois epoch of social development. The working class cannot grow strong, cannot mature, cannot consolidate its forces, except by 'establishing itself as the nation,' except by being 'national.' "[12]

Lenin's writings after the successful Bolshevik revolution refine his earlier thoughts and reflect his growing concern for individual Communist blueprints for action, tailored to the specific needs of specific nations. Lenin had always maintained that other countries should not model their socialist revolutions after the Russian experience, an experience unique to Russia because of peculiar social, economic, and political conditions. In his ongoing argument with the German Left, for example, Lenin first chides them for their stand against any form of compromise with the bourgeoisie: "Our theory is not a dogma, but a *guide to action,* said Marx and Engels; and it is the greatest crime on the part of such 'patented' Marxists . . . that they have not understood this."[13] He then states the national theory that allows MacDiarmid to declare himself a "Scottish Communist":

> The whole point now is that the Communists of every country should quite consciously take into account both the main fundamental tasks of the struggle against opportunism and "Left" doctrinairism and the *specific features* which this struggle assumes and inevitably must assume in each separate country in conformity with the peculiar features of its economics, politics, culture, national composition (Ireland, etc.), its colonies, religious divisions, and so on and so forth.[14]

Thus, when MacDiarmid specifies his Communism as Scottish and speculates upon the future of a Gaelic Commonwealth, modeled after the soviets of Russia, he speaks Leninist orthodoxy. Ironically, the "unfortunate limitations of certain leading members of the Communist Party in Scotland,"[15] alluded to in MacDiarmid's autobiography, include the failure of European Communists to know the essential works of Lenin, a failure which has prompted misunderstandings of MacDiarmid among both Scottish Nationalists and critics.

MacDiarmid's version of a Scottish Communist Workers' Republic rests, then, on a Leninist foundation. When he praises John Maclean in *The Company I've Kept,* MacDiarmid also, as is often the case in his prose, talks about himself: "But Maclean was on sound and profound Leninist lines and was quite untainted by the Trotskyist exaltation of world revolution instead of getting on with the work immediately to hand."[16] The work at hand is to avoid confusing "progressive nationalism with chauvinistic reactionary nationalism,"[17] and to move forward from the Nationalist movement, the first step in opposing British imperialism, to the establishment of a Scottish Workers' Republic. Ultimately, this republic would become the bulwark of a Gaelic Commonwealth encompassing Scotland, Ireland, Wales, and Cornwall. To understand the full significance of this final political phase, we must consider an unusual phrase much prized by MacDiarmid: the Caledonian Antisyzygy.

This curious phrase first appears in G. Gregory Smith's *Scottish Literature: Character and Influence,* which, when it was published in 1919, influenced MacDiarmid. The term describes an essential psychological condition or world view that Smith finds to be characteristic of the Scottish temperament. Its hallmark is a love for contradictions, a delight in maintaining two opposing ideas as equally true. Smith applies the term to the political, religious, and aesthetic realities of Scottish life, remarking that "in the very combination of opposites . . . we have a reflection of the contrasts which the Scot shows at every turn, in his political and ecclesiastical history, in his polemical restlessness, in his adaptability," so that we should not be surprised to find that "in his literature the Scot presents two aspects which appear contradictory."[18] In MacDiarmid's hands, this rather simple concept blooms into an almost mystical explanation for the ordering of reality; not just Scottish literature, or even Scottish politics, but all of the perceivable world becomes a vast working out of the union of opposites subsumed under the phrase Caledonian Antisyzygy. Politically, it leads MacDiarmid to the idea of the Celtic Commonwealth.

MacDiarmid intends that the Gaelic Commonwealth, or Celtic Front, will play its role in world history as one half of a cosmic antisyzygy, an idea which he expresses most fully in the essay "The Caledonian Antisyzygy and the Gaelic Idea," which originally appeared in *The Modern Scot* for July 1931. In it, MacDiarmid reviews Smith's definition of the Caledonian Antisyzygy and then applies it to Scotland's political situation with interesting results. He begins by quoting Dostoevsky to support his own interpretation of Scotland's necessary stature: "If a great people does not believe that the truth is only to be found in itself . . . if it does not believe that it alone is fit and destined to raise up and save all the rest by its truth, it would at once sink into being ethnographical material and not a great people."[19] As part of a Gaelic confederation of socialist republics, Scotland would help reestablish a disrupted balance of world power that had formerly comprised, on an international political and cultural scale, an antisyzygy in its own right. Some forty-five years before the age of Kissinger, MacDiarmid had formulated his own idiosyncratic brand of East-West detente based upon the semi-mystical expansion of the Caledonian Antisyzygy:

> We in Scotland are at the opposite side of Europe. The old balance of Europe—between North and South—has been disrupted by the emergence of Russia. How is a quadrilateral of forces to be established? England partakes too much of Teutonic and Mediterranean influences; it is a composite—not a "thing-in-itself." Only in Gaeldom can there be the necessary counter-idea to the Russian Idea—one that does not run wholly counter to it, but supplements, corrects, challenges, and qualifies it. Soviet economics are confronted with the Gaelic system . . . the dictatorship of the proletariat is confronted by the Gaelic Commonwealth with its aristocratic culture—the high place it gave to its poets and scholars.[20]

In this new East-West polarization, two significant factors emerge. First, the economic system of the Celtic Front will not be fashioned after the Soviet (or English) economic plan, but, as we shall soon see, after the Douglas plan. Second, MacDiarmid breaks with traditional Soviet Communist theory by giving thought primacy over material reality; hence, we find not a dictatorship of the proletariat but an aristocracy of poets and scholars meant to "polarize Russia effectively" by restoring the balance between "freedom and thought, which Russia is denying."[21] For MacDiarmid, this denial of thought is not in keeping with the basic tenets of dialectical materialism but a corruption of Communist thought, and specifically of Leninist thought. Despite the attack on idealism waged by Marx and Engels, in which they write, "life is not determined by consciousness, but consciousness by life,"[22] MacDiarmid interprets Leninism to mean the exaltation of idea over material reality, surely a curious line of thought in an avowed Communist. Its justification as a consistent principle lies in MacDiarmid's attempt to bring certain ideas of Lenin to completion.

In *What Is to Be Done?*, Lenin's early pamphlet on the tasks of Communism, he states a major theme of all his writings: Communism and knowledge must progress together in the socialist epoch. Lenin has much more in mind than mere technological knowledge: "Modern socialist consciousness can arise only on the basis of profound scientific knowledge. Indeed, modern economic science is as much a condition for socialist production, as, say, modern technology, and the proletariat can create neither the one nor the other, no matter how much it may desire to do so; both arise out of the modern social process."[23] Because the proletariat cannot create scientific knowledge, socialist ideology comes from without, from the intelligentsia who temporarily utilize bourgeois knowledge. But—and this is the essential fact recognized by MacDiarmid—this is a temporary state of affairs. The ultimate ideal of Communism is a state in which all of its members know all things, at least in a utilitarian sense. Thus, the division of labor will be eliminated and universal education will raise the intellectual level of all; Lenin speaks of the necessity for trade unions to develop into broad industrial unions that will proceed to "eliminate the division of labor among people, to educate and school people, give *them all-round development and an all-round* training, so that they *know how to* do everything."[24] At other times, Lenin stresses the profound depth of scientific investigation required to correctly analyze modern phenomena, an act that requires intellectual flexibility and an awareness of the constant flux in nature implied by dialectical materialism. In *Once Again the Trade Unions, The Present Situation, and the Mistakes of Trotsky and Bukharin* (25 January 1921), Lenin writes that "in order really to know an object, we must embrace, study all its sides, all connections and 'mediations' . . . dialectical logic demands that we take an object in its development, its 'self-movement' . . . in its changes."[25] MacDiarmid celebrates this approach to knowledge in the "Third Hymn to Lenin":

> Not only an analytical mind but also
> A great constructive, synthesizing mind
> Able to build up in thought the new reality
> As it must actually come
> By force of definite laws eventually,
> . . . .
> Such clairvoyance is the result
> Of a profound and all-sided knowledge of life
> With all its richness of colour, connections and relations
> Hence the logic of your speeches—like some all-powerful feelers
> Economic, political, ideological, and so forth.[26]

In *Lucky Poet,* MacDiarmid claims that Communism represents a monumental challenge to modern man, for "to be a Communist one must first master all that is of value in the whole cultural heritage of mankind. Those who have not done this are, as Lenin says, 'not Communists, but mere bluffers.'"[27] Again, in "The Politics and Poetry of Hugh MacDiarmid," written under the psuedonym of "Arthur Leslie," MacDiarmid typifies his brand of Communism by quoting from Lenin once more: "Now, for the first time, we have the possibility of learning . . .

we must utilize every moment in which we are free from war that we may learn, and *learn from the bottom up*. . . . It would be a very serious mistake to suppose that one can become a Communist without making one's own the treasures of human knowledge."[28]

MacDiarmid's Communism seizes upon one aspect of Lenin's thought in particular and draws the conclusion that ideas are the truest reality. The goal of Communism is to produce a society of thinkers in which other life processes become semi-automatic, a view which may indeed distort Leninist thought. As much as Lenin endorses the search for knowledge, he remains within the bounds of traditional Marxist theory regarding the concrete nature of reality, staunchly maintaining, in *One Step Forward, Two Steps Back* (1904), that "there is no such thing as abstract truth, truth is always concrete. [29] MacDiarmid himself pursues this line in his evolving poetry of fact. But his is also the poetry of ideas, ideas which form the universe as surely as atoms do in classical physics. The "myth" of the Caledonian Antisyzygy, like the "dynamic myth" of Dostoevsky's Russia, is enough to hold a world together. For this reason, MacDiarmid expands upon the Leninist theory of Communism and knowledge to achieve a goal outlined by Marx in *The Communist Manifesto:* "In place of the old bourgeois society, with its classes and class antagonisms, we shall have an association, in which the free development of each is the condition for the free development of all."[30]

In the key passage from "The Caledonian Antisyzygy and the Gaelic Idea" quoted earlier, we can now fill in the ellipsis to see how MacDiarmid plans to counter Soviet economics: "Soviet economics are confronted with the Gaelic system with its repudiation of usury which finds its modern expression in Douglas Economics."[31] MacDiarmid's strong and consistent backing of Major C. H. Douglas's Social Credit scheme needs some explanation. After all, Douglas himself declares that his plan is not a form of socialism: "It seems difficult to make it clear that the proposal for a National Dividend, which would enable the products of our industrial system to be bought by our own population, has nothing to do with Socialism, as that is commonly understood."[32] Indeed, in spite of that last qualifying phrase, Social Credit is capitalism blown to extraordinary proportions; the nation becomes the corporation and its citizens the coupon clippers, partakers in the newly minted wealth of a national heritage translated into money. MacDiarmid's interest in Douglas is therefore important not because of the economic theories underlying Social Credit but because of the light it sheds on MacDiarmid's larger concerns. In a revealing footnote in *Lucky Poet,* MacDiarmid observes that "as a Socialist, of course, I am, it should be obvious, interested only in a very subordinate way in the politics of Socialism as a political theory; my real concern with Socialism is as an artist's organized approach to the interdependencies of life."[33] This interest in an almost biological interpretation of the interdependencies of society is what draws MacDiarmid to the economics of Douglas. In Douglas's theories, MacDiarmid found an economic justification for the freedom of man from constant labor, a freedom which allowed the necessary leisure to think.

The crux of Douglas's economic theory is the so-called A + B Theorem. In brief, if A represents all of a nation's payments to individuals in the form of wages, salaries, dividends, and so forth, and B represents all payments made to other organizations in the form of costs for raw materials, bank charges, and other external costs, then the cost of a product so produced must be equal to A + B, or the cost of manufacturing. However, only A, which does not by itself equal A + B, represents actual purchasing power; an amount of purchasing power equal to B must therefore be injected into the economy. The result: bank credit. In order to fill the gap between prices and purchasing power, the financial system of a nation, controlled by the banks on both national and international levels, creates money. The act of allowing bank overdrafts or loans means, in effect, that "the institution concerned writes a draft upon itself for the sum involved, and the general public honours the draft by being willing to provide goods and services in exchange for it."[34] Such a loan involves credit "of which no one, not even the banker, except potentially, has the money equivalent."[35]

Another result of the A + B Theorem is that a producing nation, in order to find outlets for its goods that will absorb its surplus (remember that no single nation can buy all of its production), engages in the struggle for foreign markets. And so the financial system of the modern world is the prime irritant in creating international friction. Therefore, as Douglas writes in *The Monopoly of Credit,* "if we recognize this, we shall be in a better position to realize that we are never at peace—that only the form of war changes."[36] Indeed, Douglas's approach to war is Marxist in its orientation: "Military war is an intensification of economic war, and differs only in method and not in principle."[37] Lenin had analyzed the relationship between finance capital and war in similar terms: "The question as to whether these changes are 'purely' economic or *non*economic (for example, military) is a secondary one, which cannot in the least affect fundamental views on the latest epoch of capitalism. To substitute the question of the form of the struggle and agreements (today peaceful, tomorrow warlike, the next day warlike again) for the question of the *substance* of the struggle and agreements between capitalist associations is to sink to the role of a sophist."[38] Both Douglas and Lenin are concerned with revealing the underlying causes of international unrest, not the secondary local irritants of economic depression and war. Both find it in the financial systems of Western Europe and America. Furthermore, Douglas traces the origin of crime itself and social maladjustments like alcoholism to the financial system under which we labor. In *Social Credit,* he connects the financial system of Western Europe to a civil law network that is based upon outmoded religious concepts involving rewards and punishments. Again, the relationship to Marxist thought seems clear:

> Even crimes of passion take their origin, in the majority of cases, from physiological or psychological reactions which can be traced back to economic or financial causes. The world is full of organizations for the suppression of such social evils as inebriety and prostitution. The financial origin of the latter hardly needs emphasis, but it is not so generally recognised that habitual industrial overstrain, long hours, and insanitary conditions of work, and the excessive indulgence in alcoholic or other artificial stimulation, are almost invariably found in one and the same geographical locality.[39]

Finally, because man is "rewarded" for work and "punished" for not working, and because, despite a technology that should result in fewer man-hours of labor, the financial system requires ever-expanding markets, the system "exalts industrial work to an end in itself, and deplores, as one of the major evils of the time, the leisure which it labels 'the unemployment problem.'"[40]

The answer, of course, is to reform the financial system in order to create channels for distributing goods equitably, to redefine "unemployment" (with its negative moral and ethical connotations) as "leisure," and to share the real capital of the state among all its members in the form of national dividends. As shareholders in, instead of debtors to, the state, citizens would be paid "(1) a small and decreasing share due to his individual efforts, and (2) a large and increasing amount due to his rights as a shareholder or an inheritor, or if it may be preferred, a tenant for life of the communal capital." The result of such a scheme is a revolutionary and never before realized freedom that allows a measure of individuality not available under either capitalism or Communism: "Not being dependent upon a wage or salary for subsistence, he is under no necessity to suppress his individuality, with the result that his capacities are likely to take new forms of which we have so far little conception."[41]

MacDiarmid praises Douglas and promotes his economic theories as a basis for a new Scottish economy in *The Company I've Kept,* in a revised section of that book in his *Selected Essays,* in *The Scottish Scene,* and whenever he has a chance to debate economics. But in *Lucky Poet,* he lets fall a recollection by Eric Linklater that demonstrates the real value of Major Douglas to MacDiarmid. Linklater recalls that, after denying any interest in the increase of wealth that might accrue under the Douglas plan, MacDiarmid had exclaimed, "I have no interest whatsoever in prosperity"—upon which Linklater adds that he had "the uncommon impression that here was a man who advanced an economic theory for purely aesthetic reasons."[42] This is an extremely accurate remark, as MacDiarmid himself recognized. Just as the "proprioceptive" theories of the maverick psychologist Trigant Burrow, based upon the consideration of man as a biological phylum responding physiologically to his environment, had intrigued MacDiarmid,[43] so did Douglas's concern for the social cohesiveness of man that found expression in biological terms. In Douglas's thinking, man is "kept in agreement with dogmatic moral and social ideals . . . by arranging that they shall be kept so hard at work that they have not the leisure or even the desire to think for themselves."[44] As a result, their minds are totally absorbed in the drudgery of work which should, in a technologically advanced age, be an automatic process like breathing, like the pumping of the heart and the endless flowing of blood. In *Social Credit,* Douglas explicitly equates man's economic pursuits with biological functions:

> So far from the mere sustenance of life through the production of food, clothing, and shelter from the elements being, with reason,

> the prime objective of human endeavour, it should now be possible to relegate it to the position of a semi-automatic process. Biologists tell us that the earliest known forms of life devoted practically the whole of their attention to the business of breathing. Breathing is not less necessary now than it was then, but only persons suffering from some lamentable disease pay much attention to it.[45]

The present financial system is a "lamentable disease" that forces its organisms to be painfully aware of processes which should be automatic. Again, in *The Monopoly of Credit,* Douglas reemphasizes the nature of his theory, claiming that "Business" should cease to be "the major interest of life and would, as has happened to so many biological activities, be relegated to a position of minor importance, to be replaced, no doubt, by some form of activity of which we are not yet fully cognisant."[46] MacDiarmid repeats this theme in a poem that could just as easily be called "Second Hymn to Douglas" as "Second Hymn to Lenin":

> Oh, it's nonsense, nonsense, nonsense,
> Nonsense at this time o' day
> That breid-and-butter problems
> S'ud be in ony man's way.
>
> They s'ud be like the tails we tint
> On leavin' the monkey stage;
> A maist folk fash aboot's alike
> Primaeval to oor age.
>
> . . . .
>
> Sport, love, parentage,
> Trade, politics, and law
> S'ud be nae mair to us than braith
> We hardly ken we draw.
>
> Freein' oor poo'ers for greater things,
> And fegs there's plenty o' them,
> Tho' wha's still trammelt in alow
> Canna be tenty o' them.[47]

The biological evolution of man's economic needs, the comparison of such concerns to "braith," the freeing of our "poo'ers" that we "Canna be tenty o'" as yet—all come from Douglas, not Lenin. In the Social Credit scheme, MacDiarmid saw hope for the values of "liberty, leisure, and culture" leading to the "*economic independence and complete freedom of the individual.*"[48] Douglasism is especially appealing in this respect because its tenets are based upon the recognition that "the second necessity under which men and women labour, *after the primary necessity* [survival] *has been met,* can broadly be described as the satisfaction of the artistic instinct; which can be further analyzed and defined as the incorporation in material forms of ideals conceived in the mind."[49] The vision of the future shared by MacDiarmid and Douglas contains a world in which the artistic instinct becomes the fulfillment of a primary necessity, while "breid-and-butter" problems are solved by semi-automatic, biological processes that can be depended upon not to break under the strain of economic competition.

Under the twin influences of Lenin and Douglas, MacDiarmid espouses the conscious reorganization of society along cultural and economic lines that parallel one another; a change in one necessarily implies change in the other:

> Poetry of such an integration as cannot be effected
> Until a new and conscious organization of society
> Generates a new view
> Of the world as a whole
> As the integration of all the rich parts
> Uncovered by the separate disciplines.
> That is the poetry I want.[50]

Out of the Scots tongue, MacDiarmid hoped to forge a poetry that would contribute to this new view of the world, a poetry that would address the particular crises of Scottish life, a poetry that would learn from Lenin and Douglas how to cut with a new and sharper edge into the exposed flank of English domination.

Notes

1. Hugh MacDiarmid, *The Company I've Kept* (Berkeley, Calif.: University of California Press, 1967), p. 145.
2. See Duncan Glen, "Hugh MacDiarmid: Supporting Roles," in *Hugh MacDiarmid: A Critical Survey,* ed. Duncan Glen (Edinburgh: Scottish Academic Press, 1972), pp. 12–34, esp. pp. 31–32.
3. David Craig, "MacDiarmid the Marxist Poet," in *Hugh MacDiarmid: A Festschrift,* ed. K. D. Duval and Sydney Goodsir Smith (Edinburgh: Duval, 1962), pp. 87, 97.
4. Hugh MacDiarmid, *Lucky Poet: A Self-Study in Literature and Political Ideas, Being the Autobiography of Hugh MacDiarmid* (Berkeley, Calif.: University of California Press, 1972), p. 67.
5. See Sydney Goodsir Smith, "MacDiarmid's *Three Hymns to Lenin,*" in Glen, ed., *Hugh MacDiarmid: A Critical Survey,* pp. 141–54, esp. pp. 141–42.

6. Ibid., p. 145.
7. Ibid., p. 144.
8. MacDiarmid, *The Company I've Kept,* p. 123.
9. James E. Connor, ed., *Lenin on Politics and Revolution: Selected Writings* (Indianapolis, Ind.: Bobbs-Merrill, 1968), pp. xi–xxviii.
10. Georg Lukács, *Lenin: A Study on the Unity of His Thought,* trans. Nicholas Jacobs (Cambridge, Mass.: MIT Press, 1971), p. 88.
11. *Lenin: A Reader,* ed. Stefan T. Possony (Chicago: Regnery, 1966), p. 3.
12. Ibid., p. 50.
13. *"Left-Wing" Communism, An Infantile Disorder* (April–May 1920), in Connor, ed., *Lenin on Politics,* p. 304.
14. Ibid., p. 306.
15. MacDiarmid, *Lucky Poet,* p. 232.
16. MacDiarmid, *The Company I've Kept,* p. 151.
17. Ibid., p. 134.
18. G. Gregory Smith, *Scottish Literature: Character and Influence* (London: Macmillan, 1919), pp. 4–5.
19. C. M. Grieve, "The Caledonian Antisyzygy and the Gaelic Idea," in *The Modern Scot* (July 1931), p. 151. This essay is reprinted in *Selected Essays of Hugh MacDiarmid,* ed. Duncan Glen (Berkeley, Calif.: University of California Press, 1970), pp. 56–74.
20. Ibid.
21. Ibid., p. 152.
22. Karl Marx and Friedrich Engels, from *The German Ideology,* in *Marxism and Art,* ed. Maynard Solomon (New York: Random House, 1974), p. 36.
23. Connor, ed., *Lenin on Politics,* pp. 44–45.
24. *"Left-Wing" Communism, An Infantile Disorder,* in Possony, ed., *Lenin: A Reader,* p. 293.
25. Ibid., p. 12.
26. Hugh MacDiarmid, *Three Hymns to Lenin* (Edinburgh: Castle Wynd Ltd., n.d.), pp. 20, 21.
27. MacDiarmid, *Lucky Poet,* p. 355.
28. Glen, ed., *Selected Essays of Hugh MacDiarmid,* pp. 29–30.
29. Possony, ed., *Lenin: A Reader,* p. 7.
30. Karl Marx and Friedrich Engels, *The Communist Manifesto,* trans. Paul M. Sweezy (New York: Monthly Review Press, 1968), p. 41.
31. Grieve, "The Caledonian Antisyzygy," p. 151.
32. C. H. Douglas, *The Monopoly of Credit* (London: Eyre & Spottiswoode, 1931), p. 103.
33. MacDiarmid, *Lucky Poet,* p. 241.
34. Douglas, *The Monopoly of Credit,* pp. 18–19.
35. Ibid., p. 21.
36. Ibid., p. 97.
37. Ibid., p. 99.
38. *Imperialism, the Highest Stage of Capitalism* (1916), in Possony, ed., *Lenin: A Reader,* p. 131.
39. C. H. Douglas, *Social Credit,* 3d ed. rev. (London: Eyre & Spottiswoode, 1935), pp. 79–80.
40. Douglas, *The Monopoly of Credit,* p. 110.
41. Ibid., p. 116.
42. MacDiarmid, *Lucky Poet,* p. 36.

43. See ibid., pp. 193–94.
44. Douglas, *Social Credit,* p. 115.
45. Ibid., p. 70.
46. Douglas, *The Monopoly of Credit,* p. 112.
47. Hugh MacDiarmid, *Complete Poems: 1920–1976,* ed. Michael Grieve and W. R. Aitken (London: Martin Brian & O'Keeffe, 1978), 1:325.
48. "Economic Independence for the Individual," in *Selected Essays of Hugh MacDiarmid,* ed. Glen, pp. 155, 156. This essay is a slightly revised version of one portion of the chapter "Major Douglas and Social Credit: John Maclean and the Clydesiders," in *The Company I've Kept,* pp. 104–36.
49. Douglas, *Social Credit,* pp. 108–9.
50. "The Kind of Poetry I Want," in MacDiarmid, *Complete Poems,* p. 1025.